The Ultimate

Bible Guide

for Children's Ministry

Helping Kids Make the Bible Their Lifetime Friend

Group
Loveland, Colorado

THE ULTIMATE BIBLE GUIDE FOR CHILDREN'S MINISTRY
Copyright © 1999 Group Publishing, Inc.

Credits
Contributing Authors: Karl D. Bastian, K. Christie Bowler, LaDona L. Hein, Dennis R.
    McLaughlin, Rick Osborne, Janet Colsher Teitsort
Editor: Lori Haynes Niles
Quality Control Editor: Paul Woods
Chief Creative Officer: Joani Schultz
Copy Editor: Betty Taylor
Art Director: Jean Bruns
Cover Art Director: Jeff A. Storm
Cover Designer: Becky Hawley
Cover Illustrator: Kenneth Spengler
Computer Graphic Artist: Desktop Miracles
Illustrator: Victoria Hummel
Production Manager: Peggy Naylor

Library of Congress Cataloging-in-Publication Data

The ultimate Bible guide for children's ministry.
       p.   cm.

       ISBN 0-7644-2076-3
       1. Bible--Study and teaching.   2. Christian education of children.   I. Group
    Publishing.
    BS600.2.U48   1999
    268'.432--dc21   98--45392
                                                                                                          CIP

10 9 8 7 6 5 4 3 2 1   08 07 06 05 04 03 02 01 00 99

Printed in the United States of America.

Contents

Introduction

"For the word of God is living and active."
HEBREWS 4:12A

Whether your kids are preschoolers or nearing their teens, it's never too early or too late to use the living Word of God. It's through his Word that we become friends with him. It's through his Word that we build a relationship with him. It's through his Word that we come to know what he wants for our lives.

But too often, children are "put off" from a rich interaction with the Bible because it seems like such a grown-up book, full of complicated rules and a strange numbering system. It doesn't seem "active" with its fragile, gold leaf pages and few pictures!

The ideas in *The Ultimate Bible Guide for Children's Ministry* will help kids see how the Bible lives and how they can use it actively. Your kids will need their own Bibles to use both in class and at home. Their Bibles will become remarkably similar to scrapbooks, notebooks, or workbooks as your kids learn to really *use* them. And as they do, they will begin to recognize their Bibles as friendly tools rather than distant and harsh rule books.

There are an infinite number of things you can *do* with God's Word. As your kids get a handle on its organization, they will want to dig into it and uncover its rich treasures. They will want to unravel mysteries about its people, and find out more about how its promises are for them, personally, as they go to school, attend church, and live at home. Once you get them started on this path of free exploration, they'll amaze you with their creative interactions with the living, active messages of God's great love.

There are also multiple ways to use the activities from *The Ultimate Bible Guide for Children's Ministry*. You can intersperse them throughout your regular class sessions. You can create your own "miniseries," offering four to six weeks of intensive Bible training. You can have a one day "BibleFest" for families to participate in together. Some churches present Bibles to their children when they reach a milestone. Elaborate on that tradition with an activity-filled party that will help kids really use their new gifts. What a way to celebrate a landmark in kids' lives!

So get ready to dig in and go deeper in your own appreciation of the Bible. As you teach kids, you'll find this journey is one to be undertaken heartily, learning together as you go!

Chapter One

THE INFORMATION STATION

Rick Osborne

I n this chapter, we will look at two main questions: "Why do we have the Bible?" and "Who does the Bible belong to?"

WHY DO WE HAVE THE BIBLE?

God gave us the Bible because he loves us and wants to have a relationship with us. In the Bible, God tells us who he is, his plan for the world, and how we can have a relationship with him right here, right now. You can explain the Bible to children using any of the following three analogies: God's autobiography, God's plan for the world, and God's instruction manual for life. Use one or more of the following activities with your class to help your children get a feeling for the significance of God's Word.

God's Autobiography

Say: **The Bible is God's autobiography. An autobiography is a book written by someone about themselves. All of you have a life story. In fact, when we introduce ourselves, we sometimes have to give a mini-autobiography, telling just a little bit about who we are and what we've done.**

Right now, I'd like each of you to turn to a partner and give a three-sentence autobiography to him or her. Give children about three minutes to share. Then ask:

- **How was this experience like finding out about God from the Bible?**
- **How was it different?**

One of the reasons God gave us the Bible is to tell us about himself. The Bible tells us who God is and what he thinks is important. Ask:

- **What do you think are some reasons God wants to show us who he is?**

- What types of things do you think are important to God?

Affirm children's answers, and say: **God wants to show us who he is for three main reasons. First, if we are to trust God and have a relationship with him, we need to know what he is like and what we can expect of him. Second, God created everything to line up with who he is. We need to understand his character in order to know how everything works and to have a successful life. Third, understanding who God is gives us a picture of what he wants us to be like.** Ask:

- **So what do you think God is like?**
- **Where did you get those ideas about him?**

Allow children to share their perceptions of God. Point out that the Bible tells us that God is good and that everything God does is good. It says that God is trustworthy and that he will always act with our best interests in mind. The Bible also says that God is faithful; not only is he able to do what he says he can, he will do it! So the Bible shows us that we can trust God with our lives. The Bible also says that God is love (1 John 4:8, 16). That means everything he does is based on love. Everything God asks us to do and be is because he loves us and wants the best for us.

Say: **The Bible also shows us that as God's creation, we have a lot of things in common with him.**

- **What are some traits we have in common with God?**

Let kids brainstorm ways people are like God. Write their answers on newsprint or a chalkboard. Make sure they include that both we and God have creativity, emotions, desire for relationships, sense of humor, love of beauty and wisdom, and more. Ask:

- **What are some ways God is different from us?**

Say: **The autobiographies we shared earlier were very short. Our lives could not be contained in three sentences. But they did give our neighbors a way to begin to get to know us. In the same way, the Bible is not a complete record of everything God has ever done. It is a wonderful starting point for getting to know him, and for finding out what is true about him and what is not. Because the Bible came from God, we know that what it tells us about him is true.**

An Ant's Eye View

Preparation: You'll need paper and crayons or markers for this activity.

Even the most unique and awesome things about God can be put into terms simple enough for children to understand. Use the following activity to help explain some of God's amazing characteristics.

Say: **The Bible tells us that God is amazing: He is everywhere (*omnipresent*), he knows everything (*omniscient*), and he can do anything (*omnipotent*). What do you think it would feel like to be God?** (Discuss briefly.) **Let's do something that will help us understand life from God's perspective.**

Take your students outside to an area where they can observe ants at work. After your students have studied the ants for a few minutes, have them draw pictures of what they imagine the world looks like from an ant's perspective. Perhaps they can draw pictures of themselves from an ant's perspective. Have your students show their pictures to the class and discuss what they drew and why. (As an alternative, bring in an ant farm, or have your students think of times they've watched ants at work.)

Say: **For ants, the anthill is the whole world. It is impossible for an ant to see more than a small part of the hill at a time. But we can look at an anthill and see the ants and everything around them at one glance. We can do this because we are much bigger than ants and we can see a lot farther than they can. If we told an ant about all that we can see, it would probably think that we are every-where—and to an ant, we are everywhere.**

● **How is our experience of watching ants similar to our relationship with God?**

● **How is this experience different from our relationship with God?**

After students answer, say: **We can only be in one place at one time, but God can be everywhere at the same time, and he can see everything. God's perspec-tive is much broader than ours in much the same way that our perspective is far greater than the ants'.**

Read Psalm 139:7-12. Ask:

● **What do these verses remind you about?**

● **If you were to tell an ant what life was like on the other side of the lawn, or inside our house, what would you say?**

● **What do you think the ant would think?**

Say: **Unlike us, God really does know everything. He is omniscient. God knows everything that happened in the past, everything that is happening in the present, and everything that will happen in the future. The Bible tells us this fact about God in Psalm 139:1-6.** Read the passage aloud, and then ask:

● **Why is this important for our lives?** (It means he always has wise answers for us. There's no question too difficult for him to answer, no problem too big for him to solve.)

Say: **Ants are incredibly strong for their size. They can lift objects that are many times their own body weight. But if we picked up the ant and all of his brothers and sisters and carried them to an anthill on the other side of the lawn, they might think that we could do anything. God's power is even more awe-some. There is nothing he can't do. God has the power of love, compassion, and forgiveness.** Ask:

● **Why do you think God wants us to know these things about him?** Read Romans 8:35, 37-39. (The Bible tells us what God is like so we can love and trust him.)

Say: **God is greater than we can understand, but he described himself in the Bible so that we can relate to him as our loving heavenly Father.**

WHAT IS GOD'S PLAN FOR THE WORLD?

The Bible is really one big story: It is God's plan for salvation, his love letter to the world. An understanding of the big story helps us to understand God's love and his plan to bring us back into relationship with him. It also gives us a background in which to place the smaller stories we learn about in the Bible. Too often these stories are taught without any reference to the "big picture." Most kids have heard Bible stories, but without the big picture it is difficult for them to understand how the stories relate to one another, or in what order they happened. The stories in the Bible do make sense when we study them individually, but it's important to tie everything together so kids can see God's purpose and plan everywhere in the Bible.

Get the Picture?

Preparation: Before class, write the names of some or all of the major biblical characters listed on the handout on pages 9-10 on index cards, and put a separate string through each card so it can be worn around the neck. Photocopy the "Characters" handout on pages 9-10, cut apart the quotes, and attach them to the backs of the appropriate index cards. Make sure you have at least one card per child (duplicates are OK).

This activity will help your students understand how the stories of the Bible fit together to tell the one big story of God's salvation plan.

Say: **The Bible is full of stories. These stories tell us why God made us, what happened in the past, why Jesus had to come, what is happening in God's plan today, and what is going to happen in the future. But if you put all of the stories together, they tell one big story. Let's find out how this works.**

Give each student a card to wear. Then have the students try to organize themselves in order from first to last, according to when their characters appear in biblical history. Help them if they need it. Once they are in order, have the entire group be seated. Tell them to get ready to read what's on the back of their cards when their characters appear in the following summary of the big story of the Bible. As you read the following story and say a character's name, have children who are wearing the cards of that character stand and read their cards together. This is most effective when you race through the story, running from group to group. Explain that you are attempting to cover about four thousand years in five minutes.

(The story begins on page 11.)

CHARACTERS (in chronological order)

ADAM AND EVE: "We were the first people. God gave us a beautiful garden to live in, but we disobeyed God and were sent away from him and the garden. Since then, everyone has been born sinful and separated from God. But God promised that one of our descendants would save the world from sin."

NOAH: "When God was angry at all the sinful people in the world, he chose me and my family to build an ark and to load two of every kind of animal inside. Then he caused a flood. It rained for forty days and nights! My family and the animals on the ark were the only ones who survived."

ABRAHAM: "God told me that he would lead me and my people into the land of Canaan, a land that my children would own forever. He also gave my wife, Sarah, and I a child, named Isaac, even though we were very old. God promised that one of Isaac's descendants would bless the whole world."

JACOB: "I am Isaac's son. God changed my name to Israel. I had twelve sons, who were the ancestors of the tribes of Israel. One of them, named Joseph, was sold into slavery, but he ended up second in command in Egypt because he was faithful to God and because he interpreted a dream for the king. He invited us to come to live in Egypt, and we did."

JOSEPH: "My father, Jacob, gave me a special coat because I was his favorite son. My brothers were jealous, so they sold me as a slave into Egypt. But I kept loving and obeying God, and years later God helped me explain a dream to Pharaoh. The dream predicted a huge famine. Pharaoh told me to get Egypt ready for the famine so the people wouldn't starve."

MOSES: "When I was born, my Hebrew mother hid me in a basket in the river to save me from the Egyptian soldiers who wanted to kill all Hebrew baby boys. Pharaoh's daughter found me, and I grew up in Pharaoh's palace. One day I ran away into the desert because Pharaoh was angry at me. Years later, God appeared to me in a burning bush and told me to go back to Egypt to tell Pharaoh to set the Israelites free from slavery. I did as God asked, and the Israelites were set free."

DAVID: "One day I went out to visit my brothers, who were in the army fighting against the Philistines. A giant came out and challenged us and insulted our God. I asked the king to let me fight him. Though I was just a boy, I killed the giant with only a sling and a stone. Later, God made me king of Israel and called me a man after his own heart."

DANIEL: "I am a Jew who became a leader in Babylon. I prayed to God even when it was against Babylon's law, so I was thrown into a lion's den. But God kept me safe!"

MARY: "I am a descendant of King David. One day I was told by an angel that I would have a son and that God would be his father. Later, an angel told my fiancé, Joseph, about the baby I was going to have. We believed what we were told, and it happened, and the baby's name was Jesus."

JESUS: "I am God's Son. I came to pay the penalty for people's sins and to show people the way back to God. I died on the cross and rose from the dead. Then I went up to heaven to prepare a place for the people who believe in me."

SAUL: "I did everything I could to stamp out the followers of Jesus. Then one day, Jesus appeared to me and asked why I was persecuting him. From that day forward, I became a follower of Jesus myself, and my name was changed to Paul. Some of my letters to the churches are in the New Testament."

JOHN: "I was called 'the disciple Jesus loved.' Many years later I was in exile on an island when Jesus appeared to me and gave me a message for the church. He said he would return one day to gather his believers together and take them to live with him in a new heaven and a new earth, where there will be nothing but love and happiness. In heaven, we'll be with God as his children, just as he planned before the world began. What a party that will be!"

The big story of the Bible starts when only God existed. He made everything! He made people, Adam and Eve, to be like his children. *(The students with the Adam and Eve cards read here.)*

So God sent Adam and Eve out of the Garden of Eden, away from what he had prepared for them, to let them find out that their own way couldn't work. Adam and Eve had children, who had children, who had children, and so on, until soon the world was full of sinful people. God was very sad. He knew that he had to stop people from destroying one another and somehow demonstrate that evil had grave consequences. When things couldn't get any worse, God found one man on earth who still loved him, Noah. *(The students with Noah cards read here.)*

Noah's children had children, who had children, and so on, until God called Noah's descendant Abraham and promised to be his God. *(The students with the Abraham cards read here.)*

Isaac had a son named Jacob. *(The students with the Jacob cards read here, followed by the students with the Joseph cards.)*

The Israelites, all Israel's descendants, came to Egypt and had children, who had children, who had children, and so on, until they increased, and Pharaoh got worried. He made them slaves and ordered their baby boys killed. That's when Pharaoh's daughter rescued an Israelite baby named Moses. *(The students with the Moses cards read here.)*

God sent ten plagues to show he was stronger than Egypt's false gods. In the last plague, the eldest child in every family was to die. But God told the Israelites to kill lambs and put the lamb's blood on the doorways of their homes so God's angel would pass over them. The lambs died instead of the Israelites' eldest children. This was called the Passover. That night Pharaoh let God's people go. The Israelites left Egypt in a huge group. God led them into the desert and gave Moses the Ten Commandments and the Law, telling them how to please God and have a good life. *(Have the entire group stand, count to ten, and sit back down.)*

Then God led the Israelites to the land he'd promised Abraham long ago. Under the leader Joshua, the Israelites defeated the wicked people who lived there and settled in.

When the Israelites followed God's Law, things went well. When they didn't, their enemies conquered them. They'd cry to God for help, and God would send a judge or leader to defeat their enemies.

Eventually, the Israelites asked God for a king. Their first king, Saul, fought their enemies, the Philistines. A giant Philistine, named Goliath, mocked God. The Israelite soldiers were all afraid of Goliath, but one Israelite boy wasn't afraid. His name was David. *(The students with the David cards read here.)*

David's son Solomon was wise, but later kings didn't love God as David did. God sent prophets like Isaiah, Elijah, Jeremiah, and Daniel to remind his people to follow his Law. They didn't listen. When they didn't listen to Daniel, God let enemies take them far away to Babylon as prisoners. Daniel was one of the Israelite or Jewish prisoners taken to Babylon. *(The students with Daniel cards read here.)*

Later, the ruler of Babylon let some Jews return to their land. Now some of God's people decided to obey God's Law. Everything was ready for the key part of God's plan: the birth of Jesus. *(The students with the Mary cards read here.)*

Jesus was God, but he became a person like us because he loved us. He was part of God's plan—the promised Messiah, or savior. God told simple Jewish shepherds and non-Jewish wise men about his Son's birth, showing that Jesus had come for everyone. *(The students with the Jesus cards read here.)*

Jesus grew up in Nazareth. When he was about thirty, he began the job God had given him. Jesus was baptized in the Jordan River by John the Baptist, and then led into the desert by God. Satan tempted Jesus in the desert, just as he had tempted Adam and Eve, and tried to convince Jesus to do things Satan's way instead of God's, but Jesus refused.

Jesus chose twelve men to be his special followers, or disciples. He taught them and the crowds who followed him about God and his kingdom. Jesus showed God's love by healing the sick and feeding the hungry. He taught people how to have a good relationship with God.

The religious leaders did not believe that Jesus was God, and they were afraid that the people would follow Jesus instead of them. Jesus taught that God loved the world so much that he gave his one and only Son. Anyone who believes in him won't die but will have eternal life (John 3:16). The leaders thought the key was to obey the Law, not to believe in Jesus. They decided to get rid of Jesus, but they had to be careful, because they knew that if they arrested him, they would cause a riot.

The leaders accused Jesus of saying he was God's Son. The punishment was death, according to Jewish law. They found Jesus guilty, and crucified him—a horrible death. While he hung on the cross, Jesus asked God, his Father, to forgive the people because they didn't know what they were doing. Then he said, "It is finished," and he died. He'd done everything God sent him to do.

After Jesus died, some of his friends put his body in a tomb. The Jews guarded the tomb so no one could steal Jesus' body and say he'd risen from the dead. But on the third day, the tomb was empty. Jesus appeared to many people, proving he was alive again, and then he went up to heaven. God accepted Jesus' death (instead of ours) as payment for our sins! That meant the separation begun by Adam and Eve ended. Now all people who believe can become God's children. *(Have the whole group stand and cheer and then be seated again.)*

Jesus sent the Holy Spirit to help his followers tell the world about him. The Jewish leaders tried to stop them, but it didn't work. One Jewish leader in particular, named Saul, searched out Jesus' followers to have them punished and killed. *(The students with the Saul cards read here.)*

John, another disciple of Jesus, was sent to an island prison for following Jesus. Jesus gave John a message for the church. This message is in Revelation, the last book in the Bible. *(The students with the John cards read here.)*

Have kids all trade character cards and attempt to rearrange themselves in order. Say: **Each of the events of the Bible helps us to understand God's overall plan to bring people into a relationship with him.**

LIFE'S INSTRUCTION MANUAL

Another reason God gave us the Bible was because he wanted to provide an instruction manual for life. The Bible contains everything we need to know about how to live lives pleasing to God.

If you want to live a worthwhile life, think ahead before rushing into a situation. Stop, and pull out life's instruction manual, the Bible. God gave us the Bible as a user's guide for life. And it is complete—right down to introducing us to the Manufacturer.

Life Is a Puzzle!

Preparation: You'll need jigsaw puzzles and small, unassembled Lego vehicles or other simple models (one for every five students). You'll also need pictures of the completed puzzles and instructions for the models.

This fun activity will help you reinforce the Bible's importance as an instruction manual for life.

Form groups of five. Give each group an unassembled puzzle or model. Put the instructions or picture of the finished product aside. Dump the pieces on the table, and ask your students to try to assemble the puzzle or model without looking at the picture on the puzzle box or the instructions for the model. Give them a time limit, and see how far they get. Afterward, ask:

● **What would have helped you finish with less confusion?**

● **What was it like to work without instructions?**

Ask kids to try the activity again. Ask one group to volunteer to work without the instructions or puzzle picture and one group to work with them.

Say: **One reason God gave us the Bible was to show us how life works. God designed the world according to who he is, and he knows how the world works best.**

● **How is this experience like or unlike our lives when we don't look at God's instructions in the Bible?**

● **What were the reasons some of you chose to work on the project without instructions?**

● **What might be some reasons a person would choose not to follow God's instructions?**

● **What might be some of the consequences of not following God's** instruction manual?

- What are some of the instructions you know the Bible gives?
- Why do you think God gave those instructions to us?

Say: **In the Bible, God gives us principles and guidelines for how to live happy, productive lives. Do you want a good life? Then pull out Life's Instruction Manual, follow it, and you will have the best life possible.**

WHO DOES THE BIBLE BELONG TO?

This section will examine who wrote the Bible, how it was printed, and how it was translated through the centuries until today.

THE BIBLE: A PUBLISHING MIRACLE

The Bible belongs to God. We know this because God is the only one who could have created such an amazing book. It is a publishing miracle!

The Bible is the authority on God, written by someone who knows what he's talking about: God himself. But God didn't exactly sit down and put pen to paper, or fingers to keyboard; he *inspired* the Bible. That means he "breathed into" or worked with and through people and by his Holy Spirit so that they wrote what he wanted them to write.

God was very careful about who he chose to write the Bible. Using the writers' own unique personalities, cultures, and experiences, God inspired each of them to write his message for the world. What they wrote is from God. God has breathed life into all of Scripture (2 Timothy 3:16). God chose more than forty people from very different life situations to write the sixty-six books of the Bible. These writers spoke different languages (Hebrew, Aramaic, and Greek) and lived on different continents (Africa, Asia, and Europe) and at different times—it took more than fifteen hundred years to write the Bible from beginning to end! The list includes poets, prophets, kings, prisoners, philosophers, priests, fishermen, a doctor, and even a politician or two. Most incredible of all, every one of these forty writers managed to agree on all the basic issues of faith. This could have been possible only if God was behind it all—and he was!

What Do You Think?

This activity will help your students understand how difficult it would have been for the writers of the Bible to agree on anything unless God was involved.

Hand out a sheet of paper to each student. Say: **If there are aliens, what do you think they look like?** After kids give some answers, ask:

- What are the two best desserts? TV shows? music groups?

After they answer, say: **Write down what you think are the two most important rules of life.** Have the students read their answers aloud. How many answers are the same?

Ask:

● **How many of your answers do you think would have matched your grandparents?**

● **How many of your answers do you think will match your grandchildren's in fifty years?**

When students have finished, talk about how difficult it is to get people to agree on things and how incredible it was for the biblical writers to agree on so many things, even though they were all such different people who lived in different times.

God's Wisdom or Not?

Preparation: Before class, write some verses from the book of Proverbs on slips of paper, and put them in a hat or paper bag. Also make some blank slips for kids to write on.

This exercise will help your students to understand how the Bible was put together.

Say: **The book of Proverbs contains a lot of wise sayings. Other people have written proverbs throughout history, but the Bible proverbs are special because they are inspired by God. Let's see how that might have worked.**

Have kids create their own "wise sayings" and write them on the blank slips of paper you have prepared. Fold these, and drop them into the hat or bag with the biblical proverbs.

Draw one, and read it aloud. Ask the class whether they think it is a Proverb or a student's saying. If they say the saying was written by a student, ask them who they think wrote it. Do this several times to give everyone a turn.

Discuss how easy it is to recognize God's voice and how easy it is to recognize the personality of their friends through how they write and what they choose to write about. Say: **The books of the Old Testament were passed down by the Jews from generation to generation as sacred writings. Ninety years after Jesus' birth, a Jewish council officially recognized the Old Testament as it is preserved today. The New Testament books were written by the apostles—or people who knew them—after Jesus' death and resurrection. Other writings about Jesus were not included in the New Testament. The church leaders of that day had to decide which books and letters were inspired by God and which were not.**

● **What things do you think they considered before accepting a writing?**

● **How do you think they made their decisions?**

Say: **The council used several considerations. One was whether the writer was someone who was called to be an apostle by Jesus or who worked closely** with the apostles. Another test was to see whether the book was accepted and used by the church as a whole, and yet another was to see whether the people of God recognized the Holy Spirit speaking through the text. These decisions were made final a little more than three hundred years after Jesus' death and resurrection. No more books can ever be added to the Bible.

THE BIBLE: A PRINTING MIRACLE

The Bible is not only a publishing miracle, it's a printing miracle as well. The story of how God's Word was copied and recopied, translated and retranslated is amazing.

If we believe that the Bible is God's Word, then we must believe that the same God who loved us enough to inspire it was able to deliver it to us the way he wanted it to be delivered. If you were going to leave a very important message for someone, you would probably make sure that you'd written it clearly and put it in a safe place so the person would be sure to see it. That's just what God did!

The Bible is the best-kept ancient book in the world. Some of its earlier sections, such as the Pentateuch (the first five books of the Old Testament), were written thousands of years ago. Even the newest books of the New Testament were written nearly two thousand years ago. Although the copies of the original biblical texts that exist today are really old, they are still only copies of copies of copies, and—you get the picture. So how can we know if they're accurate? Rest assured. God raised up groups of people, called scribes, who dedicated their lives to making sure that God's Word was accurately preserved for the generations to come.

The Hebrew scribes treated the Old Testament with tremendous respect. They had a lot of rules and guidelines to follow when copying the Old Testament. For instance, they counted the words and letters of each book and of the Old Testament as a whole and then compared the numbers from their copies to those of the originals. If there was even one error, the copy was destroyed and the scribe started again. Needless to say, the scribes tried to get things right the first time!

The scribes had very specific rules about transcribing the Scripture, including what type of ink and parchment or papyrus to use, how to space the words, and so on.

The New Testament was copied with similar attention to accuracy, but the rules followed by the Christian monks who did the copying were not quite as strict as those followed by the Hebrew scribes. Monasteries had rooms, called scriptoriums, which were especially made for copying the Scriptures, among other things.

We know the scribes did a good job because when we compare copies of the biblical books from various times and places, they're nearly exactly the same! For example, until 1947, our oldest piece of the Old Testament was from eight hundred years after Jesus' time. Then a shepherd boy in Israel found clay jars hidden in a cave. The jars contained what we call the Dead Sea Scrolls. Among them was a scroll of Isaiah from two hundred years before Jesus! People compared this manuscript with what we already had—it's almost exactly the same!

The Telephone Game

This game will give your students an idea of how difficult it was for the scribes to ensure that God's Word survived uncorrupted over the centuries.

Say: **Making sure that God's Word was accurately copied throughout the centuries was a huge challenge. The "Telephone Game" gives us an idea of how difficult that job was.**

Have everyone sit in a circle. Have one student whisper a message into the ear of the person to his or her left, such as, "The four gospels, Matthew, Mark, Luke, and John, were directed to different audiences so that all could be introduced to the Messiah." That person whispers the message, as he or she heard it, to the person on his or her left, and so on around the circle. The last person then tells the group the message as he or she heard it. Usually the last message is practically incoherent and may have nothing to do with what was originally said. Play the game two or three times.

Say: **This game takes only five minutes; imagine trying to do the same thing over thousands of years! But the Bible scribes didn't just tell the story to one another, they passed it on in writing. Let's see how this works.**

Pass out a small piece of paper to each student. Have the first student write a short made-up proverb and then pass it on to the next student. Tell the second student to try to copy the proverb as carefully as he or she can, making sure to match both the content and the form of the first student's writing. The copy should be identical to the original, like a photocopy. The second student will pass his or her copy to the third student, and so on around the circle. When the exercise is finished, have the last student read aloud the final copy to see if it matches the original. Have the students look at all the copies together to see if they can spot any changes in the wording, spelling, or style of writing. When they are finished, say: **This is exactly how the scribes copied and recopied the Bible through the years.** Ask:

● **Considering your hard work of copying, how many ancient copies of the Bible would you guess we have?**

Explain that we have more than five thousand ancient, handwritten copies or parts of copies of the New Testament, and tens of thousands of copies of the Old Testament. The next best-kept ancient document, in terms of how many copies we have and how soon after the original they were made, is a story called the Iliad by a Greek writer named Homer. There are only 643 known copies of the Iliad, and the oldest was made five hundred years after the original.

The original manuscripts of the New Testament, the Gospels (Matthew, Mark, Luke, and John), which tell about the life of Jesus, were written less than fifty years after Jesus died. We don't know of any originals that still exist. We do have a manuscript that contains almost all of the New Testament and dates from only three hundred years after the last book of the New Testament was written, as well as a manuscript that may be slightly older and contains nearly the entire Bible.

The oldest portion of a New Testament manuscript we have today contains a few verses of the Gospel of John, copied onto a piece of papyrus no more than seventy, and perhaps as little as twenty, years after John first wrote it. Ask:

● **What do these facts tell you about the care of the Scriptures?**

● **What other thoughts do these facts inspire about how God has protected his Word?**

Say: **Those are some of the reasons the Bible is known as the greatest publishing miracle in history!**

THE BIBLE BELONGS TO US

Although the Bible belongs to God, he has given it to us.

Everyone can read the Bible, but we make it our own only when we put God's Word into practice. The book of James reminds us that just saying we'll do something is not the same as doing it. By our actions, we show that we are serious about our words. In the same way, we show that we are serious about our beliefs by putting them into practice.

Translated Into Many Tongues

Preparation: Photocopy the various translations of John 3:16 on page 20 for your students.

This exercise will give your students an idea of how the Bible looks (and sounds) in other languages.

Say: **God's Word is for everyone! Today we have several English language translations of the Bible, including the New International Version (NIV), the New King James Version (NKJV), the New Revised Standard Version (NRSV), the New American Standard Bible (NASB), and the New Living Bible, among others.**

At least part of the Bible has been translated into more than 2,100 languages all over the world. The whole Bible has been translated into more than 275 languages, and more translations are being made.

Give students a photocopy of the "John 3:16" handout on page 20. Have kids choose a partner, and let them have fun trying to pronounce these words and figuring out what languages they are in. Have them create their own language translation in the eighth box. After about ten minutes, have partners say the verse according to their translation to the whole group.

Ask:

● Why is it important for people to have the Bible in their own language?

● What can be done for people who don't have the Bible in their own language?

● How can you help others understand God's Word when they don't read it?

Say: The Bible has a message for people who speak all different languages. It is God's book, given to us all.

JOHN 3:16

1. "For God so loved the world that he gave his one and only Son, that whoever believes in him shall not perish but have eternal life."

• •

2. "Allah begitu mengasihi dunia sehingga diberikanNya AnakNya yang tunggal, agar semua orang yang percaya padaNya tidak mati tapi mempunyai hidup yang kekal."

• •

3. "Isten úgy szerette a világot, hogy egyetien gyermekét adta, hogy aki hisz benne, el ne vesszen, hanem örök élete legyen."

• •

4. "Dios amó tanto a la gente de este mundo, que me entregó a mí, su único Hijo, para que todo el que crea en mí no muera, sino que tenga vida eterna."

• •

5. "Deus amou o mundo de tal maneira, que deu o seu único Filho, para que todo aquele que nele crer não morra, mas tenha a vida eterna."

• •

6. "Dieu a tellement aimé le monde qu'il a donné son Fils unique, afin que tout homme qui croit en lui ne meure pas, mais qu'il ait la vie éternelle."

• •

7. "Maana Mungu aliupenda ulimwengu hivi hata akamtoa Mwana wake wa pekee, ili kila amwaminiye asipotee, bali awe na uzima wa milele."

• •

8. _____

_____

_____

• •

(Answers: 1. English, 2. Indonesian, 3. Hungarian, 4. Spanish, 5. Portuguese, 6. French, 7. Swahili.)

THE BIBLE IS AMAZING

I hope that after reading this chapter and sharing it with your students, you and your pupils are convinced that the Bible is truly a one-of-a-kind book. It is God's book, and it was written in a way that no ordinary book could have been written and still make sense. In addition, its contents have been accurately preserved through thousands of years in a way that no other book's contents ever have.

If there were such a thing as a Book Hall of Fame, the Bible would hold the number one spot.

It's the Number One Bestseller of All Time. The Bible has been read by more people, in more languages, than any other book. Millions of copies and portions of copies are distributed worldwide each year.

It's the Most Accurate: Remember, if we compare the number of really old existing copies of the Bible with the copies of other ancient books that still exist, we find that the Bible has been translated more carefully than any book ever written.

It Tells Us How It Was: Since the Bible was first written, people have claimed it was inaccurate because, they said, there was no proof that the people and some of the places the Bible talks about ever existed. In fact, archaeologists (scientists who study the artifacts of ancient civilizations) continue to find things that support the Bible's accuracy. For example, people didn't believe that Sodom and Gomorrah and other cities mentioned in Genesis 14 ever existed in the Jordan Valley. But ancient tablets have been discovered that list the same cities in the same order as they are found in Genesis 14. There are dozens of other examples of archaeology confirming the validity of the biblical record.

It Tells Us How It Will Be: The Bible not only tells us about the past, it tells us about the future through the use of prophecy. Prophecy is God telling us what is going to happen in the future, sort of like the weather forecaster predicts what kind of day it will be tomorrow—only God is always right! Many biblical prophecies have already come true. Isaiah predicted the coming of Jesus hundreds of years before Jesus was born (Isaiah 53).

So, as you can see, the Bible is no ordinary book. The fact that it exists at all is so extraordinary that no other book is even in the contest.

But God wants the Bible to be part of your kids' Hall of Fame, too, and you can help that to happen as you continue to explore God's Word together.

Chapter Two

BIBLE USE BASICS

Karl D. Bastian

The Bible is a BIG BOOK. Young children who are used to reading books all the way through in a few minutes before bed may be discouraged from opening it for themselves. Children need to learn that, despite its great size, the Bible can be read, understood, and can become a regular part of their lives. Rather than being a book just for grown-ups, the Bible can be every kid's book too.

This chapter contains a collection of teaching tips that will help kids with the basics of Bible use. Your kids will learn that committing some of these basics to memory is a tool to help them use their Bibles effectively, not just a chore imposed by "that's-no-fun" adults. You'll teach children how the Bible is organized, the order of the books, and how kids can find their way around in this giant collection of God's greatest messages—messages they can decode and follow!

"Kids in the Word" Rap

Here is a "rap" you can use to get your students excited about reading and learning about the Bible. It can be performed by puppets, leaders, or kids themselves—but wearing shades is a must!

Haven't you heard?
We're kids in the Word.
We're studyin' the Bible,
And we don't think it's absurd.

We think it's rather awesome;
We think it's rather cool.
If you're not readin' it and heedin' it,
Then you may be a fool.

'Cause life with God is awesome;
It's what it's all about.
That's why we get excited,
And that's why we sometimes *SHOUT.*

The Bible's filled with facts,
And it's filled with fun.
It's filled with lots of stories
Of the things that God has done.

But not just things that happened
So very long ago,
It's got lots of help for now
If you take the time to know.

So if you see me with my Bible,
Don't call me a nerd.
It's the coolest of the cool
To be a Kid in the Word.
A Kid in the Word,
It's the coolest of the cool
To be a Kid in the Word.

BREAKING IT INTO BITE-SIZE PIECES

The Bible is actually a collection of smaller books. The word "Bible" literally means "books." These many books are divided into two main divisions, the Old Testament and the New Testament. The Old Testament is like Part One of God's Plan for Salvation. The New Testament, Part Two, completes this plan. It is so perfect that there will never be a need for a Part Three. The goal of all of the following activities is to get kids so familiar with the strange-sounding names of Bible books and their locations that they are no longer intimidated by the Bible's vastness, but instead will see the Bible as an approachable friend.

Testament Tangle

Here is a fun game that will help children review which books are in which testament.

Clear a large area. Divide the room down the center with two lines of masking tape about five feet apart. Form two teams—the Old Testament team and the New

Testament team. Have each team stand on one of the two lines, so they are facing each other.

Say: **I'll call out the name of a book of the Bible. If it's a New Testament book, the New Testament team will try to tag anyone on the Old Testament team as the Old Testament team members turn and try to reach the wall behind them. Once the Old Testament team members reach the wall, they are safe. But if someone gets tagged, that person must join the other team. If I call out an Old Testament book, that team tries to tag the others.**

Kids have to think fast about which testament the books are in. Hesitation or the wrong assumption will put them on the new team to continue playing. Play along with the kids to help model positive team spirit and to give kids who may not know the books yet a clue about which way to run. Play until everyone is on the same team, or until time is up.

Off the Wall

Preparation: Write each book of the Bible on a piece of construction paper. Hang a banner on one wall that reads, "Old Testament," and another on the opposite wall that reads, "New Testament."

TEACHER TIP

You can facilitate checking for accuracy by using a color pattern. For example, write Genesis on yellow construction paper, Exodus on red, Leviticus on white, Deuteronomy on blue, and Numbers on orange. Then repeat the pattern with successive books so that kids can see where there are errors.

As children arrive, give each one a sheet of construction paper with a Bible book written on it. Instruct them to tape their papers to the wall labeled with the testament that book is found in. They may come back for another Bible book after they have placed the first one. After all the books are posted on the walls, work together to place the books in the correct order.

When there is disagreement, have kids use their Bibles' table of contents to look up the correct order. When looking up references during your lesson, have kids point to the book on the wall to reinforce what testament the book is in and where it can be found.

THE BIBLE'S ORGANIZATION

The Bible is a very organized book. Its structure has been described in several ways. Each accurately describes the layout of the Bible, but with a different emphasis.

The first, and most common, is the Library Model. The Library Model groups the books of the Old and New Testaments into eight groups or divisions. The Old Testament divisions are Law, History, Poetry, and Prophecy. The New Testament divisions are Gospels, History, Letters, and Prophecy.

Bible Stack Attack

Preparation: You'll need sixty-six old magazines, cereal boxes stuffed with newspaper, rectangular blocks, or discarded books. Tape the boxes shut, and make a cover for each. Write the name of one Bible book on the "spine" or front cover of each.

STACK ATTACK GAME #1

Race against the clock to see how quickly the group can stack the entire Bible in order. First, play the game by placing Genesis on the floor first, and then for a greater challenge, have kids stack the books in reverse order, so that Revelation is on the floor and Genesis is on the top. You may also choose to stack one testament at a time.

STACK ATTACK GAME #2

On the floor, in the center of the room, mix up all the books. Set up two tables on opposite sides of the room. Label one table "Old Testament" and the other "New Testament." On each table, place four labels with the divisions for that testament, if you are teaching this model. (The "Old Testament" table would be divided into Law, OT History, Poetry, and OT Prophesy; the "New Testament" table would be divided into Gospels, NT History, Letters, and NT Prophesy.) On "go," have children grab books from the mixed-up pile and race to place them in the correct stack on the correct table. Have available a chart or a Bible table of contents for kids to check if they are unsure where to place a particular book. For an extra challenge, encourage kids to stack the books in order within each category.

STACK ATTACK GAME #3

After removing *one* book, place the remaining books in one stack. When you shout "go," the group must try to determine which book is missing. Kids may move the books around to figure it out. Encourage kids to place the books in smaller groups to aid them in determining which is missing.

A second way to look at an overview of the Bible is to think of it as the story of a journey from law to grace. The Old Testament contains the "Stories of Law," and the New Testament contains the "Stories of Grace." Each can be divided into four segments:

STORIES OF LAW

Law (Genesis-Ruth)
Kings (1 Samuel-Esther)
Poetry (Psalms-Song of Songs)
Prophets (Isaiah-Malachi)

STORIES OF GRACE

Jesus (Matthew-John)
Church (Acts)
Letters (Romans-Jude)
Future (Revelation)

Bible Book Scramble

This game can be used with either of the models above, and works great within a camp setting or other times you have a large group. The more kids the better—this game is at its best with sixty-six kids or more, one for each book with additional kids on any books. If you do not have sixty-six or more kids, then use only the Old Testament books (thirty-nine) or New Testament books (twenty-seven) or assign random books to children so that the whole Bible is represented. For Bible divisions with a small number of books, such as New Testament prophesy, assign every book so that every division is well represented.

Have children sit in chairs in a circle. Assign a book to each child, as described above. Have one child stand in the middle of the circle of chairs. Remove his or her chair from the circle.

The person in the center will call out the name of a division of the Bible. All children who have a book in that division must leave their seats and find new chairs to sit in while the person in the center tries to reach one of the empty chairs first. The person who is left without a seat becomes the caller in the center of the circle.

For extra fun, the caller may choose to call out "Scramble." Then *every* child must leave his or her seat to find another.

Ten Questions or "I'm Thinking of a Bible Book"

Choose a leader who will think of one book of the Bible. The children will then take turns trying to determine which book the leader is thinking of by asking questions that the leader can answer only with a "yes" or "no." If a student receives a "yes" answer, he or she may ask another question and may continue to ask questions until a "no" answer is given. Then another child may ask a question. In order to guess the book in ten questions or less, children will need to learn to use the testament and division breakdowns to narrow their choices. For example, if the book is Proverbs, they might first ask, "Is it in the Old Testament?" "Is it one of the prophets?" "Is it a book of poetry?" "Is it Psalms?" "Is it Proverbs?" (Yes. And in only five questions, too!)

Older children with significant Bible knowledge may enjoy playing this game by basing their questions on content rather than placement of Bible books.

Sixty-Six Seconds or Less

Here's a great game for those extra minutes at the end of class. You've heard of *60 Minutes*. This game takes less than sixty-six seconds. You'll need a stop watch, or at least a watch with a second hand. Say: **Remember that in order to find Bible verses, it really helps to know the order of the books of the Bible. In this game, you will say one book of the Bible, beginning with Genesis, and then move on in order—anyone on the team can shout out the next book of the Bible. The only rule is that no one person can shout out two books in a row.** Let the entire group try to beat its best times.

What Book Am I?

Tape the name of a Bible book to each child's back. Then have the whole group roam around the room asking others yes or no questions to help them discover which Bible book each of them has. Each person may ask only one question of another at a time. Once someone has correctly guessed his or her book, that student may continue roaming to answer other people's questions. The game is over when all players determine their Bible books.

Memorizing the books of the Bible in order will allow kids to access God's Word quickly and effortlessly. While memorizing takes work, it doesn't have to be dull or boring! It can be fun. Here's a fun way to teach the books of the Bible absolutely pain-free.

Bible ABCs

Take advantage of kids' familiarity with the "ABCs" song by using its tune as the tune for books of the Bible. The letters of the alphabet are included to help you follow the original tune.

OLD TESTAMENT

A B C D = **Genesis, Exodus,**
E F G = **Leviticus, Numbers,**
H I J K = **Deuteronomy, Joshua,**
L M N O P = **Judges, Ruth,**
Q R S = **First and Second Samuel,**
T U V = **First and Second Kings,**
W X= **First and Second Chronicles,**
Y Z = **Ezra, Nehemiah,**
Now I know my = **Esther, Job,**
ABCs = **Psalms and Proverbs,**
Won't you come = **Ecclesiastes,**
and sing with me? = **and the Song of Songs,**
Q R S = **Isaiah, Jeremiah,**
T U V =**Lamentations, Ezekiel,**
W X = **Daniel, Hosea, Joel,**
Y Z = **Amos, Obadiah,**
Now we've sung = **Jonah, Micah,**
our ABCs = **Nahum, Habakkuk,**
We don't have time = **Zephaniah, Haggai,**
to sing it again. = **Zechariah, Malachi.**

NEW TESTAMENT

A B C D E F G = **Matthew, Mark, Luke, John, Acts, Romans,**
H I J K = **First and Second**
L M N O P = **Corinthians,**

Q R S = **Galatians and Ephesians,**
T U V = **Philippians, Colossians,**
W X = **Two Thessalonians,**
Y Z = **and Two Timothys,**
Now I know my = **Titus, Philemon,**
ABCs = **Hebrews, James,**
Won't you come = **Two Peters, Three Johns,**
and sing with me. = **Jude, and Revelation.**

HIT A BOOK BLOCK?

Getting hung up on the order of some books? Try these memory boosters to help kids remember the books of the Bible. These are mnemonics, meaning that the first letters of each word are also the first letters of the books you are trying to memorize. Remember using "Empty Garbage Before Dad Flips" or "Every Good Boy Does Fine" to learn the lines of the treble clef? That's the idea behind these memory tools.

Do not try to teach all these mnemonics, but have them "on hand" when students need a tool to help them remember.

Genesis, Exodus, Leviticus, Numbers, Deuteronomy
Remember: **Go Eat Lettuce Not Donuts.**

All the prophets in order can be memorized with this silly sentence (or make up your own):
I Just Let Eddy Drink His Juice And Overheard John Mention Now How Zebras Have Zany Manners.

Matthew, Mark, Luke and John?
Remember: **Many Men Love Jesus.**

Galatians, Ephesians, Philippians, and Colossians
Remember: **Go Eat Pop Corn.**

Have the children make up their own memory boosters. By the time they get the sentence figured out, they just may know all the books. Just for fun, here's one children's ministry's mnemonic for the entire New Testament: **"Make my life just a righteous, cool, great, enthusiastic, powerful, creative testimony to the people hearing jaws proclaim Jesus just rose."**

Mime Mania

Links are always most effective when children generate them for their own use. Have children try to come up with their own mimed memory link for each book, but use these examples for backup when kids can't think of one on their own. You can also use these as hints when kids get stuck on remembering the books. These are better than just giving the answer as they require students to think and come up with the answer themselves—which means they are learning, not just repeating what you say. The first time you use mime memory joggers, you may need to explain (or have them explain!) why or how the motion represents the book. In the future, they will usually remember what book you are hinting at.

OLD TESTAMENT

Genesis: "On your mark; get set..." They say, "Genesis."

Exodus: Wave good-bye, as though you are *exiting*.

Leviticus: Turn your back to the child as though you are *leaving*.

Numbers: Count on your fingers.

Deuteronomy: Hold *both* hands as if they are each holding a microphone, and hold one microphone toward the child as though you are singing a *duet*.

Joshua: Point to your jaw; then your shoe.

Judges: Straighten your body stiffly, and pound with an imaginary gavel as if you are a judge.

Ruth: Hold fingertips together over your head to form a "roof."

1 or 2 Samuel: Hold up one finger and then two, and then tilt your head, close your eyes, and snore because God woke Samuel up while he was sleeping.

1 or 2 Kings: Hold up one finger and then two, and then form a crown over your head with your fingers.

1 or 2 Chronicles: Hold up one finger and then two, and then point to your watch (or to your wrist if you are not wearing one) since "Chron" means "time." The first time you explain this motion, tell kids that another term for watch is "chronometer" because it is a meter for time, and that Chronicles are the books of the "times" of the Jews.

Ezra: Draw a Z in the air with your finger; then act as though you're holding a pompom for a "rah."

Nehemiah: Point to your knee; then to yourself as in *"knee-my-a."*

Esther: Make an S with your finger; then growl with an "Rrrrr."

Job: Pretend to dig with a shovel as in working at a "job."

Psalms: Hold your hands in the form of a book, and look up toward heaven with your mouth open as if singing praise to God.

Proverbs: Point to your temple to symbolize wisdom/knowledge.

Ecclesiastes: Pantomime an "eek," as though you have spotted a mouse; then make a "nasty" face, as though you have tasted something bad.

Song of Songs: "Sing" while drawing a heart in the air with both pointer fingers, as this book is about love.

Isaiah: Point to your eye, and then move your fingers as if they are a talking mouth, and then open your mouth as though someone is looking at your throat—as in *"I say ah."*

Jeremiah: Draw a letter J in the air with your finger, tap your temple, point to yourself, and then tap your temple again—as in *"Je-r-uh-my-uh."*

Lamentations: Give a short "baa."

Ezekiel: Wave your hand forward and make a face as if saying, "that's easy."

Daniel: Hold your hands together as if praying, look up (to God), and then pantomime a lion.

Hosea: Pretend to be squirting a hose; then show an expression of "Ahhhh."

Joel: Stand and salute like a soldier, or "GI Joel."

Amos: Form an A with your hands straight and your fingers touching and your thumbs extended and touching to form the little stroke in the middle of the letter; then flip your fingers, nails to nails, to form an M.

Obadiah: Draw a large O in the air, and then pretend to drop dead for *"O ba die uh."*

Jonah: Hold up one finger with your left hand (Jonah), and then open and close the fingers on your right hand to form a "fish" mouth that "swallows" Jonah.

Micah: Indicate with your thumb and pointer finger something tiny, or microscopic.

Nahum: Hum a tune while shaking your head "no."

Habakkuk: Turn your back, and take a few steps backward—as in "ha-*back-up.*"

Zephaniah: Draw a Z in the air, point to your hand, and "neigh" like a horse.

Haggai: Hold your arms up with your palms out, thumbs touching to form an H, and then point to your eye.

Zechariah: Point to a chair, and say, *"Zat chair all right?"*

Malachi: Gesture as if you are turning a key and then putting it into an envelope to *"Mail a key."*

NEW TESTAMENT

Matthew: Extend your arms straight in front of you, and then move them apart to form a flat "mat" in the air.

Mark: Draw a check "mark" in the air

Luke: Form binoculars with your hands, and *look* at the kids.

John: Draw a J in the air, and then put your hands to your cheeks with mouth open as if saying, "oh no!"

Acts: Make a chopping motion as if using an "ax."

Romans: Pretend to be "rowing" a boat.

1 & 2 Corinthians: Hold up one finger and then two, draw a C in the air, and then point up and down in an arc to show "in."

Galatians: Put your palms together to rest your head; then point to your shins—for "Gal-*lay-shins.*"

Ephesians: Draw an E in the air, and then point to your shins.

Philippians: Pretend to be pouring water from a pitcher into a cup to show *"fill-up-*ians."

Colossians: Cup hands to the sides of your mouth as if you are calling out to someone, and then point to your shins—to show *"call-all-shins."*

1 & 2 Thessalonians: Hold up one finger and then two, and then hug yourself to show *"this-alone-ians."*

1 & 2 Timothy: Hold up one finger and then two, and then point to your watch and pretend to sip tea—to show *"time-o-tea."*

Titus: Pretend to be straightening a "tie"; then wave your arm to indicate "us."

Philemon: Wave your arms as though flying; then pretend to hold your lapel to show *"fly-man."*

Hebrews: Pretend to be dunking a tea bag to show "*he brews*" tea.

James: Pretend to play guitar, as though you are jamming.

1 & 2 Peter: Hold up one finger and then two, and then pretend to be petting a pet.

1, 2, & 3 John: Hold up one finger and then two and then three, and then perform the same pantomime as for John above.

Jude: Hold up your thumbs as if you are saying, "Hey, Dude."

Revelation: Spin around as if you are making revolutions.

FINDING A VERSE

Because the Bible has a unique style of organization, it can be confusing to kids. Many of them haven't yet mastered the use of a simple period, and we ask them to deal with colons! Here are some tools to help your kids as they learn this unique code.

Eye of the Spy

Preparation: Dress up as "Secret Agent B" who explains the "Bible Code." Wear a trench coat, shades, a fedora hat, and even a badge with a B on it. (B is for Bible.) Each child will need a Bible and a copy of the Code Bookmarks found on page 34. You will need to explain the abbreviations and reference system to the children. Also make a poster or overhead that says:

Book Chapter: Verse
John 3:16
The book of John, third chapter, and sixteenth verse

Say: **I'm here to recruit agents for Operation B-I-B-L-E. Before you volunteer, it's important that you understand the significance of "The Code," otherwise known as "The Reference." The code will explain where you are to go, sort of like an address or map to a Bible verse. Without understanding the code, you'll be lost. To find a verse, you must first go to the book within the "Big Book." Secret agents must know the book may be coded with only the first few letters of its name. Here are the standard abbreviations used for Bible books.** Pass out the photocopies of the Code Bookmarks with abbreviations found on page 34.

Say: **Once you have found the book, you are almost there. Now look at the first number following the name of the book. That number is the chapter you need to turn to in that book. You'll find the chapter numbers at the top of each** page of your Bible. Look down the page, and find the big number in the text where the chapter actually starts. After the chapter number in the reference, there is a colon. This is like a flashing light to get your attention. It signals you to look down the page for the tiny numbers in the Bible text. If you see a dash between two numbers, that means you are to read all the verses including the ones pointed out by the numbers. As you explain, refer to your poster or overhead.

Have the kids demonstrate their understanding of the code by looking up several verses. Encourage them to keep their Code Bookmarks in their Bibles for quick reference.

Secret Agent Bible Search

Form two teams. Only two Bibles are needed. Give a Bible to the first person on each team. Call out a Scripture reference, preferably one that relates to some aspect of the lesson you are teaching. The first person on each team will find the Bible book and pass the Bible to the next person on his or her team. The second person will locate the chapter and pass the Bible to the next person who will locate the verse. The next person will read the verse aloud. Play will continue with the next person in line starting out with the Bible.

For a variation, form teams of four and rotate the responsibilities of book, chapter, verse, and reader. Occasionally call out, "Agency Upset," so that the teams have to reorganize before the next reference is called out. This keeps the "balance of power" equalized, giving no one team a consistent advantage or disadvantage.

BIBLE SEARCH TIP:

pen to the very middle of your Bible (this will usually be Psalms); then go in the direction necessary.

GENESIS ....GE	NAHUM ....NA
EXODUS ....EX	HABAKKUK ....HAB
LEVITICUS ....LEV	ZEPHANIAH ....ZEP
NUMBERS ....NU	HAGGAI ....HAG
DEUTERONOMY ......DT	ZECHARIAH ....ZEC
JOSHUA ....JOS	MALACHI ....MAL
JUDGES ....JDG	MATTHEW ....MT
RUTH ....RU	MARK ....MK
1 SAMUEL 1SA	LUKE ....LK
2 SAMUEL 2SA	JOHN ....JN
1 KINGS 1KI	ACTS ....AC
2 KINGS 2KI	ROMANS ....RO
1 CHRONICLES 1CH	1 CORINTHIANS 1CO
2 CHRONICLES 2CH	2 CORINTHIANS 2CO
EZRA ....EZR	GALATIANS ....GAL
NEHEMIAH ....NE	EPHESIANS ....EPH
ESTHER ....EST	PHILIPPIANS ....PHP
JOB ....JOB	COLOSSIANS ....COL
PSALMS ....PS	1 THESSALONIANS ..1TH
PROVERBS ....PR	2 THESSALONIANS ..2TH
ECCLESIASTES ......ECC	1 TIMOTHY 1TI
SONG OF SONGS ......SS	2 TIMOTHY 2TI
ISAIAH ....ISA	TITUS ....TIT
JEREMIAH ....JER	PHILEMON ....PHM
LAMENTATIONS .....LA	HEBREWS ....HEB
EZEKIEL ....EZE	JAMES ....JAS
DANIEL ....DA	1 PETER 1PE
HOSEA ....HOS	2 PETER 2PE
JOEL ....JOEL	1 JOHN 1JN
AMOS ....AM	2 JOHN 2JN
OBADIAH ....OB	3 JOHN 3JN
JONAH ....JNH	JUDE ....JUDE
MICAH ....MIC	REVELATION ....REV

CODE

Chapter: Verse

Chapter Three

BIBLE TOOLS

K. Christie Bowler

The Bible is such a simple yet profound and endlessly complex book that it would take a lifetime of study to plumb its depths. Fortunately, those who have the skills and training to do that share their studies with us in the form of Bible study tools.

These tools act as guides, leading us deeper into the amazing treasure-filled warehouse of God's Word. This Bible warehouse is packed with books, papers, pictures, and artifacts containing wisdom, history, poetry, and prophecy arranged in a seemingly random order: A story about David is tucked between pages on kingship and praise. You could spend hours hunting through the shelves for it, or you could go to a warehouse directory, put together by archivists through years of studying and cataloguing the contents. Bible tools are like that directory. They help us find our way through the Bible to the item we want.

As soon as kids know how to alphabetize (most third-graders are quite proficient in this skill), they can begin to use Bible tools to help them learn more about living the Christian life. And instead of being a drag, these tools can help uncover exciting clues that will lead your young explorers to a richer understanding of the mysteries of God's Word.

Find the Treasure

Preparation: Hide three bags of treats around your learning area. Each bag should contain at least one treat per child. Make sure you hide at least one bag where the children won't easily find it. Draw easy-to-follow maps showing where each bag is hidden.

Say: **The Bible is full of treasures for us. Some treasures seem to be hidden. I've hidden bags of treats around the building. I won't tell you how many.**

In a minute, we're all going to search. When you find a bag, you may take one treat out, but you may not tell anyone else where you found the bag. You'll have five minutes to search.

When the time is up, ask:

● How easy is it to find things when you don't know how many there are or where to look?

● Could you have found all the treats if you knew how many there were?

● What if you had maps showing where they were?

Post your maps where everyone can see them. Say: **Now you have two minutes to find any treat bags you didn't find before. When you've finished, you should each have three treats.** After the children have found all their treats, ask:

● **How much easier was it to find the treat bags when you knew how many there were and could use the maps?**

When children agree that the further information was helpful, say: **The Bible has all kinds of treasures hidden in it for each of us, just like the treat bags. But how can we know if we've found them? We need more information and "maps" to show us where to look. Bible tools, like the information and map that helped you find your treats, help us find God's treasures in the Bible.**

TOPICAL INDEX

WHAT IS IT?

A topical index groups passages alphabetically by the subjects they deal with, listing key passages in the order they occur in the Bible. Many children's Bibles include a topical index in the back.

WHEN WOULD YOU USE IT?

You would use a topical index when you want to know what the Bible says about a subject. Rather than searching through the Bible yourself or looking up a variety of words in a concordance and then sorting them for relevance, you can go to a topical index where that work has already been done.

HOW DO YOU USE IT?

Just look up the topic alphabetically. Then read each listed passage carefully.

Sift and Sort

Preparation: You'll need a topical index; two different size sieves for every eight children; two bowls per group; paper or pans for sorting; three items of different sizes (one that won't fall through any sieve, two that will fall through the big sieve, and one to fall through the smallest sieve)—for example, salt, rice, and sunflower seeds; or water, sand, and pebbles; or salt, tiny M&M's, or small candy and mints. (As an incentive to sort before eating, the best combination might be two things the children may eat mixed with something, like salt, they wouldn't eat.) Thoroughly mix the three, and divide the mixture into bags or bowls, one per group.

Form groups of eight or fewer children.

Say: **A topical index of the Bible sorts passages by topic so we can study the topic easily. Let's find out why we would use a topical index. I'll give you a bowl with three things all mixed together, sort of like topics in the Bible are mixed together. You may have a verse that talks about love next to a verse that talks about obedience, next to a verse that talks about friends. Let's call the biggest item we're sorting "love," the middle-sized item "obedience," and the smallest item "friends." We want to find out about friends today. Your job is to find all the "friends" parts in our mixture and put them together.**

Give each group a bowl of mixed items. Let the children sort by hand for a couple of minutes. When you can see they're getting frustrated, say: **There must be an easier way. What if we found a tool to help us?** Distribute the sieves. Show them how to hold the sieves in layers, with the large-holed sieve on top and the smaller-holed sieve below it. Choose a volunteer to hold the sieves while you pour the mixture through. By the time the mixture has passed through the two sieves, it will be sorted into the individual components. Shake the sieves to speed the process. Then let the children try it. Say: **The topical index is like layers of sieves, one on top of the other, so that when the Bible is poured through them, all the verses are sorted into groups with other verses like them.**

If you have chosen an edible mixture, let the children enjoy the treats. As they eat, ask:

- **What were the benefits of using the sieves?**
- **What might be the benefits of using a topical index?**

Let the kids thumb through the topical index to check their ideas.

Topic Travel

Preparation: Photocopy the excerpts from the "Topical Index" handout on page 39 (one for each child).

Say: **Let's find out what the Bible says about friends. Imagine having to sort all the Bible verses into topics by yourself before you could learn what it says about friendship! Wouldn't it be great if we could find the main verses about friends in one place? A topical index is the tool we can use to make this job simpler. Let's look at what the Bible says about friends.**

Form groups of four. Choose a Seeker, a Writer, a Reporter, and a Reader. Make sure each group has a Bible. Give each child a photocopy of the "Topical Index" handout. Say: **This is a topical index with the main passages on friends or friendship. The Seeker will look up the passages; the Reader will read what the Bible says. The Writer will write the answer you find on the question blank, and the Reporter will explain to the rest of us what your group learned. Try to answer these questions.** Assign one or more of the questions at the bottom of the topical index to each group. At the end of the activity, encourage children to keep the handout inside their Bibles to remind them how to use a topical index.

BIBLE DICTIONARY

WHAT IS IT?

Like a regular dictionary, a Bible dictionary is organized alphabetically and explains what words mean, but it explains what they mean in the Bible. So "flesh" might mean someone's muscles and skin in a regular dictionary, but in a Bible dictionary, it means our sinful nature. A Bible dictionary also explains things and countries that no longer exist. When the Bible was written, there were no televisions, cars, airplanes, telephones, public schools, or feet or inches. The world was different. The people who wrote the Bible used words that were as common to them as inches, radios, and jets are to you. But we don't use them. Who was Baal or Molech? What are Ur, Goshen, bushels, and city gates? Bible dictionaries tell us what the old words mean.

WHEN AND HOW WOULD YOU USE IT?

You would use a Bible dictionary any time you're not sure about a word you find in the Bible or when you want to know more about what a word means, what a nation or person was like, or what the Bible says about a doctrine or belief. Just look up the word, and read the article.

TOPICAL INDEX

ANDREW: Mark 1:16-18; John 1:35-44; 6:8-13

FRIENDSHIP: Exodus 33:11-17; 1 Samuel 18:1-4; 23:16; Psalm 25:8-15; Proverbs 17:17; 27:10, 17; Ecclesiastes 4:9-12; John 15:12-15; Acts 9:23-27; 11:22-26

HEAVEN: Mark 12:24-27; John 6:38-40; 14:2-6; Acts 7:56; 2 Corinthians 5:1-10; 1 Thessalonians 4:14-18; Revelation 21:1-4

JOY: Nehemiah 8:10; Matthew 5:1-12; Philippians 4:4-9; James 1:2-18

LOVE: John 13:34-35; 15:12-17; Romans 8:28-39; 1 Corinthians 13; 1 John 4:7-21

OBEDIENCE: Leviticus 26:3-17; Ephesians 6:1-3; Titus 3:1-2; Hebrews 5:8-9; 1 Peter 2:13-17

TRUTH/HONESTY: Proverbs 23:23; 24:26; Matthew 5:33-37; John 8:31-32; 14:6; Ephesians 4:25-32; 2 Timothy 2:15-16

Questions

- How does a friend help his or her friend?

- Who were some best friends in the Bible?

- When can friends stop caring about each other?

- What do friends tell each other? Can we be friends with God?

Strange Words

Preparation: You'll need a Bible dictionary; Bibles; craft items such as play-dough, paper, glue, craft sticks, and crayons. Write on a chalkboard or flip chart this list of crazy words: zorfindel, blatschmat, foonzinger, hallabang, didicomp, vizenvox, krakenpict.

Say: **Imagine we've just discovered an ancient paper with words on it we've never seen before. What other word would you like to add to this list?** Brainstorm crazy words. Add them to the list. Say: **Let's figure out what these words mean. It's** *possible* **that zorfindels help hungry kids find ice cream. Blatschmats** *might* **be catlike creatures that fly and sing. But we're not sure. Help me imagine what the rest are. Everyone choose a word from the list. Using the craft materials, make what you think that word is.** This should be a no-holds-barred, creative, fun time. When they've finished, ask:

- **Would someone know from the name what your thing was?**

Let the children name their creation, show it, and explain what it is or does. Say: **Many words familiar to the people in the Bible are almost as strange to us as some of these. It's hard to know what they meant. But Bible dictionaries give us the names and definitions so that we can better understand the Bible.**

Let the kids thumb through the Bible and find an unfamiliar word. Then look up the meaning of the word in a Bible dictionary to demonstrate how it works.

Define the Word

Preparation: You'll need paper and pencils, photocopies of the excerpt from the "Bible Dictionary" handout on page 41 (one per child). List the words from the excerpt on the chalkboard or flip chart: bath, cupbearer, homer, lots, lyre, mercy, Og, seal, timbrel, yoke.

Draw the children's attention to the words on the chalkboard or flip chart. Say: **These words are from the Bible. When the Bible was written, everyone knew what they meant. How many do you know? Choose two or three, and write what you think each word means, or draw a picture of what you think it may have looked like.** Let children share their concepts.

Say: **OK. Let's see how close you were to the biblical definitions of these words. Compare your definition to what it really means in the Bible. Here's a page with the real definitions. The words are arranged alphabetically just as they are in a Bible dictionary. Find your words, and read the definitions.** Hand out the Bible dictionary excerpts. When the children have found their words, ask:

- **How many got the right biblical definition?**

Bible Dictionary

BATH: a unit for measuring liquids; about five and one-half gallons.

BLESSED: happy, fortunate. God blesses people. We are blessed when we obey and seek God.

CUPBEARER: a very trusted officer who tasted a king's wine before serving it to the king. This was to prevent the king from being poisoned and to make sure the wine was good.

FRIEND/FRIENDSHIP: someone who loves and respects another person; someone you are close to and can trust.

HEAVEN: God's home. There's no pain, hurt, sorrow, or crying in heaven. God's people will live with God in heaven forever.

HOMER: a unit for measuring dry materials; about a donkey load.

HONESTY: being truthful all the time.

JOY: the happy feeling of being right with God and people. It depends on God, not circumstances.

LOTS: pieces of bones, sticks, or stones that were thrown like dice to help someone make a decision. God made the lots show what he wanted so the people would know what he wanted them to do.

LOVE: a deep feeling of affection and liking for someone; wanting the best for them. God is love. The more we know God, the more we'll know and have love.

LYRE: a small musical instrument with strings, something like a harp.

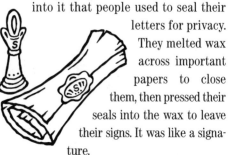

MERCY: kindness and forgiveness, more than what's fair. God has mercy on us and treats us much better than we deserve. We should have mercy on people too.

OBEDIENCE: doing what we are asked or told to do. Jesus said we'll obey God if we love him.

OG: a king of Bashan. He ruled sixty cities. He was a giant; his bed was thirteen feet long and made of iron!

SEAL: a tool with a design or writing carved into it that people used to seal their letters for privacy. They melted wax across important papers to close them, then pressed their seals into the wax to leave their signs. It was like a signature.

TIMBREL: a musical instrument similar to a tambourine.

YOKE: a wooden frame for the necks of two animals, usually oxen. It joins them together so they can pull a plow.

Say: **If we read the Bible and don't understand the words, we might get the wrong meaning. That could be confusing. Bible dictionaries help us better understand Bible words.**

Encourage children to slip the handout into their Bibles to remind them how to use a Bible dictionary as they study the Bible on their own.

CONCORDANCE

WHAT IS IT?

A concordance alphabetically lists Bible words with their references. Beside each reference is the phrase in which the word occurs. In the phrases, only the first letter of the word you're looking at is used. Hint: Use a concordance for the Bible version you're using. One version might use "loving-kindness" where another uses "mercy." If you look up "mercy" in a concordance that uses "loving-kindness," you won't find what you want.

WHEN WOULD YOU USE IT?

Often we know what we're looking for but can't remember the reference. Where is the story of Noah or Samson? Where is "blessed are the meek"? A concordance helps us find the verse quickly. We look up the word we know and go through the list of references. Since the concordance gives phrases, it's easy to find the one we want. Also, we use this tool for word studies. By reading the verses where the word is used, you can see what God says about it.

HOW DO YOU USE IT?

You look up the word you're interested in, and read through the phrases to find the one you want. Look up any verse that sounds interesting.

Once Upon a David

Preparation: You'll need papers, pens or pencils, one highlighter for every two children, and photocopies of the "Once Upon a David" short story handout on page 44, (one for every two children). On the top of each handout, write one of the following words in a circle: shepherd, wolves, God, Goliath, sling, army, Philistine, or lion.

Hand out the short story to each child. Say: **Here is a story about David before he was king. We're going to make a tool to more easily study this story. We'll call it a concordance. On the top of your page is a word in a circle. Working as pairs,** your job is to make a concordance for that word. That means every time you see your word, you'll mark it with the highlighter. Then you'll write the chapter, verse, and phrase it's in. Make a list on the paper. Show kids how by doing one of the words together.

When the children have finished, say: **Pass your concordance to the younger person in the pair to your right. Don't share your concordance with your partner. We're going to see how much help a concordance is. I'll ask questions about the words. If you have the concordance for that word, use that. If you don't, find the answer by reading the story. When you have the answer, raise your hand.** Use these questions, either asking them for each word separately or varying them between the words, depending on the time available:

● **How many times does** [word] **appear in the story?**

● **What chapter and verse does** [word] **appear in last?**

● **What chapter and verse does** [word] **appear in first?**

● **What chapter and verse does** [word] **appear in the third time?**

● **The second time** [word] **is used, what is happening?**

● **Why were some people able to find the answers so quickly?**

● **How could that help you in searching for something specific in your own Bible?**

The people with the concordance should find the answers more quickly. Say: **Concordances save us hours of time finding verses. They help us discover how words are used in the Bible and what they mean.**

Find the Verse Search

Preparation: You'll need photocopies of the "Sample Concordance" handout on page 46 (one per child), small chocolate candies, and Bibles. Look up and mark in *your* Bible the verses from the concordance so you can easily find them.

Say: **Let's see how a concordance helps us find verses in the Bible. I'm going to read a verse. See if you can tell me where it's found. If you don't know it by heart, get your Bibles out and look.** Read John 3:16. Psalm 23:1, or other verses your kids are familiar with. Then read Matthew 5:3-5 and 28:19-20. Ask:

● **What tool could we use to locate these verses?**

Hand out the sample concordances. Say: **Let's try again. Let's do a "Find the Verse Search." It will be a speed search where we are all winners: I'll read the verse, and you try to actually find it in the Bible without knowing the refer-ence. When I read the verse, look in the concordance for** *(continued on page 45)*

TEACHER TIP

This is a multiple-skill activity best suited to your older students after they've had some initial introduction to using a concordance.

Once Upon a David

1 Long, long ago, David was a shepherd boy. He stayed with his sheep in the fields overnight, just he and the sheep. ²As a shepherd, it was David's job to protect his sheep from animals like wolves, bears, and lions. ³But David wasn't afraid. He knew that his God was strong and powerful. His God would protect him. ⁴So David sat under a tree with his harp and made up songs to God, telling him how much he loved him.

2 One day, a lion attacked the sheep. David grabbed his sling and some stones and ran at the lion. ²He put a stone in his sling and whirled it around and around his head. Then he let it fly! The stone went straight for the lion's side. Whack! The lion roared in anger. David shot another stone. ³The lion decided David's sheep were too much trouble. He slunk off into the night. ⁴David had protected his sheep as any good shepherd would.

3 Another day, David's dad sent David to take some supplies and a message to his brothers. They were fighting with King Saul's army against the Philistines. ²When David arrived at the soldiers' camp, he heard a loud voice mocking the Israelites. A huge giant called Goliath was shouting up at the camp, ³"Come out and fight like men. Send your champion. I'll beat the living daylights out of him and feed him to the wolves. I'll show you that the Philistine god is stronger than the Israelite God."

⁴David knew that his God was much stronger than any false Philistine god. So he said, "I'll go fight him." ⁵He took his sling, grabbed some stones, and went down to the valley.

⁶Goliath laughed at him. "You're just a kid! Do you think you can fight a trained warrior? Come, and I'll feed you to the dogs and wolves."

⁷David said, "My God will help me. I will defeat you, and then our army will defeat the whole Philistine army."

4 David put a stone in his sling and whirled it around his head. Then he let it fly! ²Whack! The stone hit Goliath right between the eyes! He fell like a stone. ³The Philistine army saw that their champion was dead. They turned and ran, and King Saul's army completely defeated them.

⁴David visited with his brothers, then, with his harp and sling, went back to being a shepherd.

an important word from the verse. You'll find some Bible references in the concordance that use that word. Beside the Bible reference is the part of the verse the word's in. Read through the parts of the verses to find the one that matches what I read. Come to me, and get a piece of chocolate candy as soon as you know the right reference. When the children understand your instructions, choose one of the verses you have previously marked and read it aloud.

After you've gone through several verses, ask:

● **What are some situations in which you might need to find a verse without knowing the reference?**

● **How could a concordance be helpful?**

● **What other ways might you use a concordance?**

If kids don't mention it, point out that a concordance can be very useful if someone asks them what the Bible says about certain ideas, much the same way a topical index can help. It can also help them figure out whether an idea is really in the Bible or comes from another source.

What a Character!

Preparation: Prepare photocopies of the "Topical Index" handout on page 39 and the "Sample Concordance" handout on page 46 (one for each child).

Form groups of three to five. Say: **Let's see what we can learn about some of the characters in the Bible by using our Bible study tools. I'm going to give you a "Topical Index" handout and a "Sample Concordance" handout. I'll tell each group the name of a character from the Bible. Use your tools to learn something about him or her. Then, as a group, you'll perform a short skit about a key event from your character's life.** Assign each group one of the following characters: Andrew, Deborah, Jacob, Mephibosheth, Philip, Rahab, or Stephen. When the groups are ready, have them present their skits to the class. Ask:

● **Did you learn more about your character or a character from another skit?**

Say: **Remember, what the skits showed us isn't everything about that person. Other verses in the Bible talk about these people too. But usually, we learn more about something when we have sought out the information on our own than when someone just tells us. That's one reason studying the Bible for ourselves is important. Bible tools, including the concordance, help us get a complete picture of Bible characters, as well as other things in the Bible.**

Sample Concordance

baptize/baptized

Matthew 3:11 he will b you with the Holy Spirit
   28:19 b-ing them in the name of the
Acts 8:16 b-d into the name of

blessed

Psalm 41:1 B is he who has regard for the weak
Proverbs 28:20 a faithful man will be richly b
Matthew 5:3-5 b are the poor in spirit...b are
   those who mourn...b are the meek...
Acts 20:35 more b to give than to receive

Deborah

Genesis 35:8 Now, D, Rebekah's nurse died
Judges 4:4 D, a prophetess...leading Israel
   4:9 D said, "I will go with you."
   5:1 D and Barak...sang this song

disciples

Matthew 28:19 go and make d of all nations
Luke 14:26 he cannot be my d
John 13:5 began to wash his d' feet
   13:35 all men will know you are my d if you love

friend/friends

Proverbs 16:28 gossip separates close f
   27:6 faithful are the wounds of a f
Matthew 11:19 a f of tax collectors and

heaven/heavens

Genesis 1:1 God created the h
Psalm 19:1 h declare the glory of God
Matthew 6:9 Our Father in h
Philippians 3:20 our citizenship is in h
James 5:12 do not swear—not by h or earth

Jacob

Genesis 25:31 J replied, "First sell me your
   birthright."
   27:19 J said to his father, "I am Esau your
   firstborn."
   32:24 J was left alone, and a man wrestled
   35:22 J had twelve sons
Malachi 1:2 the Lord said, "Yet I have loved J"

joy

Proverbs 15:20 wise son brings j to his father
John 15:11 my j may be in you...your j may be
   complete

Galatians 5:22 fruit of the Spirit is love, j

love

Leviticus 19:18 l your neighbor as yourself
Deuteronomy 6:5 l the Lord your God with all
   your
Matthew 5:44 l your enemies
John 3:16 God so l-ed the world that he gave

Mephibosheth

2 Samuel 4:4 Jonathan had a son...name was M
   9:11 M ate at David's table
   16:4 All that belonged to M is now yours.
   19:30 M said to the king, "Let him take
   everything"

obey/obedience

1 Samuel 15:22 to o is better than sacrifice
Matthew 8:27 the winds and waves o him!
John 14:23 loves me, he will o my teaching
Acts 5:29 "must o God rather than men!"

Philip

John 1:43 Finding P, he said to him, "Follow me."
Acts 8:26 angel of the Lord said to P
   8:38 P and the eunuch...P baptized
   8:39 the Spirit of the Lord suddenly took P

Rahab

Joshua 2:1 a prostitute named R
   2:3 sent this message to R
   6:25 Joshua spared R the prostitute
Hebrews 11:31 by faith the prostitute R...
   welcomed the spies
James 2:25 even R the prostitute considered
   righteous

Shepherd

Psalm 23:1 The Lord is my s
Matthew 9:36 like sheep without a s
John 10:11 I am the good s. The good s lays down
   his life

Stephen

Acts 6:8 S, a man full of God's grace
   6:15 S...face was like the face of an angel.
   7:59 were stoning him, S prayed
   22:20 blood of your martyr S

BIBLE ATLAS/MAPS

WHAT IS IT?

Sometimes we need a tool to help us become familiar with the lands of the Bible and to orient ourselves spatially. Many Bibles provide maps. If yours doesn't, a Bible atlas can be helpful.

The maps in Bible atlases show the areas the Bible talks about. Most Bibles have maps showing the lands and cities of the Old Testament including Egypt, the areas of the Exodus, the land of the Canaan peoples that Israel conquered, David and Solomon's kingdom, and the kingdoms of Israel and Judah. The New Testament maps show the Jewish lands in Jesus' time and the areas of the Roman Empire Paul traveled. Often they include maps of cities like Rome, Corinth, or Jerusalem.

Bible atlases and maps are arranged in the order of events as they occurred in the Bible. Indexes are found in the back of the Bible and list alphabetically the place names with their page, map number, and area.

WHEN WOULD YOU USE IT?

Use a Bible atlas to find places you're reading about. Some of us are more visually oriented than others. We like to see where places are on a map or want to get a visual idea of distances and directions. When we want to know where a city is, how far Jesus walked, where Paul traveled, or where the temple was, a Bible atlas is the place to go!

HOW DO YOU USE IT?

Look up the place names in the alphabetical map index. Maps are broken into sections vertically and horizontally. The spaces between the lines are labeled. When you look up a town name, you'll find a page or map number and, often, a letter and number combination, such as "E6." Turn to the map or page listed, and look on the edges of the maps for the letters and numbers. The place you want will be in the E6 square, just as it would be in a map of your city or country.

Size It Up

Preparation: Enlarge and photocopy onto transparent overhead projector sheets the maps of Israel and New Jersey found on page 48. You'll also need copies of the map of the United States on page 49 and scissors .

Put the map of Israel on the overhead. Say: **Most Bible events took place in what is now the country of Israel in the Middle East. The Israelite spies walked all over it. The Israelites conquered it with God's help. King David ruled it. Later others conquered it. Jesus walked through it.** Ask:

● **How big do you think it is compared to the United States and our state?** Let children guess. They'll probably guess Israel is much larger than it is.

Say: **Israel is actually fairly small.** Lay the map of New Jersey on top of the map of Israel. Say: **New Jersey is the third smallest state. It's almost exactly the same size as Israel, although Israel is longer and narrower.**

Let children cut out the state of New Jersey from the photocopies of the United States map and place that land mass within other areas of the country they are familiar with. Encourage them to make connections based on their own experience, such as "Israel would fit between our church and the state line."

NEW JERSEY   **ISRAEL**

UNITED STATES

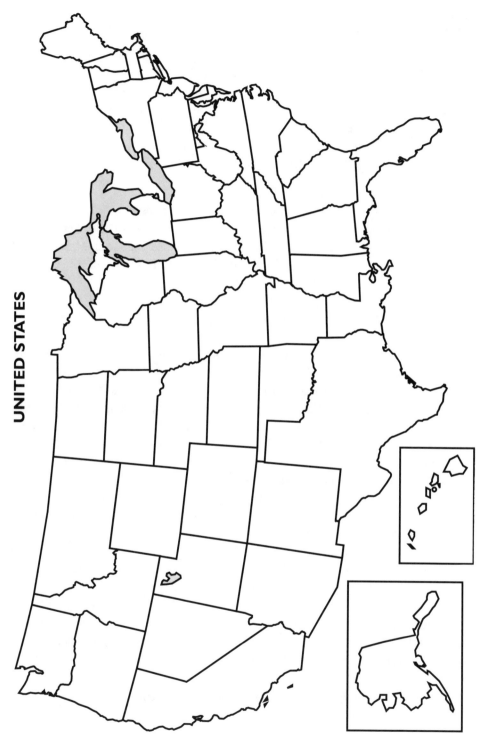

Walk It Out

Preparation: Make an overhead transparency of the map showing Jesus' travels from page 51. Measure a variety of distances using your car odometer. Begin at your building. Go around the block or to a nearby park. Map out a walk of fifteen to thirty minutes for children, depending on your time allotment. (Most healthy adults can walk three miles an hour at a steady pace.) Find landmarks or towns approximately fifteen to thirty miles from the church. Find two towns eighty to one hundred miles apart that children will know.

Ask:
- **How far could you walk in a day?** Let children guess.

Say: **Let's find out. Don't walk too fast. Remember, we have to keep up our speed for a whole day!** Lead the children outside and along the course you mapped out. When you return to the facility or reach your destination, tell the children how long it took them and what the distance was. Ask:
- **What would it be like to walk like that all day?**
- **What would you need to do to keep up your strength?** Let them suggest taking rests, stopping to eat or drink, and so on.

Say: **Let's do some math. If we walked ten hours a day, with fifteen-minute breaks every two hours, and took an hour for lunch, we'd walk for about eight hours. In that time, we'd travel** [number] **miles.** (Do your math. If you walked fifteen minutes, multiply the distance by four and then by eight to get the daily travel distance.) Say: **That's as far as it is from here to** [name a nearby town or landmark that far away]. **We could drive there in half an hour! In the Bible, there were no cars, so everyone traveled by foot or donkey. Every time Jesus walked from Galilee to Jerusalem, he walked eighty to one hundred miles! That's from** [names of two towns one hundred miles apart]. Ask:
- **How long would it take Jesus to walk to Jerusalem if he walked as fast as we did?** Let the children figure it out, dividing one hundred by how far you could walk in a day. It should be from four to six days.

Say: **But Jesus couldn't walk straight there. Let's look at the map.** Put the map showing Jesus' travels on the overhead. Say: **In those days, Jews didn't like to travel through Samaria. So the roads went around it. That meant the journey was even longer.** Point out Samaria, and show how the main road goes around it, adding miles to the journey. Say: **Tools like Bible atlases help us understand details of Bible life that are related to the land. Besides distance, what else can we learn about land?**

Give children an opportunity to synthesize their understanding of geography and what it might mean to understanding the Bible.

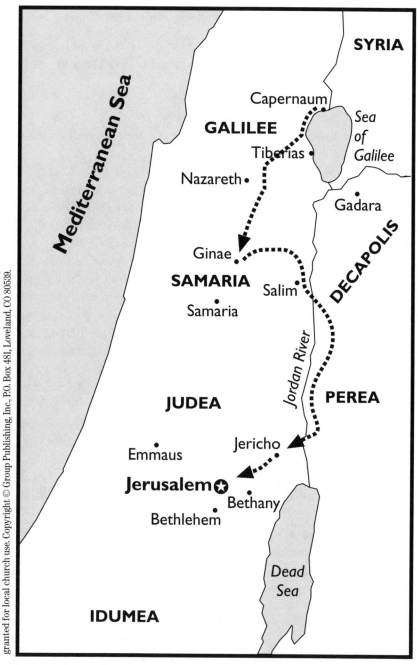

SYRIA

Capernaum

GALILEE

Sea of Galilee

Tiberias

Nazareth

Gadara

DECAPOLIS

Ginae

SAMARIA

Salim

Samaria

Jordan River

JUDEA

PEREA

Jericho

Emmaus

Jerusalem

Bethany

Bethlehem

Dead Sea

IDUMEA

Mediterranean Sea

·········▶ Jesus' last journey to Jerusalem

Down and Out

Preparation: Photocopy the relief map on page 53 (one per child).

Give each child a copy of the map on page 53. Say: **Since we live so far away from Israel, we miss out on some of Jesus' stories. Like the story of the Good Samaritan.** Ask:

- **Where was the man in the story going?**

If they can't remember, read Luke 10:30. Ask:

- **What did Jesus mean by "going down from Jerusalem to Jericho"?**

Say: **Let's look at our maps.** Ask:

- **What do you notice about the countryside?** Let children puzzle it out. If they don't understand the features, explain how the topographical lines work.

Say: **Jerusalem is in the hills, and Jericho is more than half a mile lower, near the Dead Sea! So the man really did go** *down* **to Jericho.** Ask:

- **What about Nazareth? Where is it? and the Sea of Galilee?**

Put the map of Judea in Jesus' time back on the overhead. Point out main locations children will recognize: Jerusalem, Jericho, Nazareth, Bethlehem, the Sea of Galilee, Caesarea, and others. Say: **Maps like these help us understand more about the Bible and what life was like in Bible times.**

Have kids make up several geographic statements similar to "down to Jericho" based on the topographical information they find on the map. Ask:

- **How could these ideas help us when studying the Bible?**

You may wish to point out that Bible maps can help us get a better visual picture of biblical events, as though we were really there!

OTHER TOOLS: HANDBOOKS AND COMMENTARIES

WHAT ARE THEY?

These are tools that help us delve deeper into the meaning of Bible books, chapters, and verses. They give information like who wrote each book and when, the main themes, and so on. Handbooks provide background information on the Bible itself and on the cultures and peoples it refers to, often with pictures. They bring in relevant nonbiblical sources.

Commentaries are in-depth studies, usually from the original languages, Hebrew, Greek, and Aramaic. They tell us how certain words were used and what they meant in the context of that chapter and verse.

RELIEF MAP

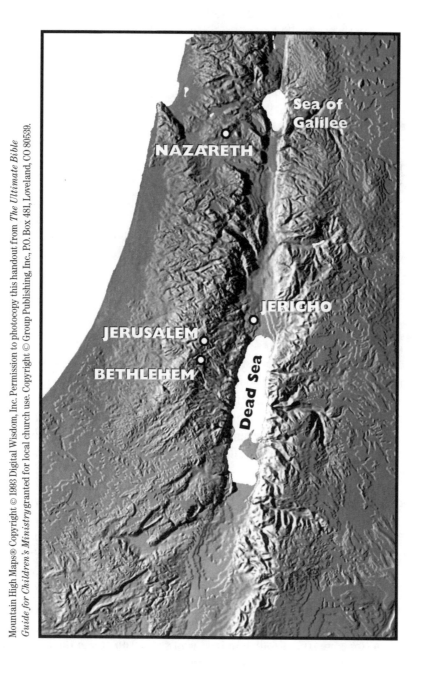

Not only did Bible writers use words and names we aren't familiar with, their lives and culture were different from ours. Most people were shepherds, farmers, or craftsmen. They knew about early and late rains, the character of sheep, and how clay pots were made. Most of their towns were inside walls. They even told time differently than we do! So, when we read a teaching story the people of that day understood, we only understand part of it. But tools like Bible handbooks or commentaries show us what the story meant back then and help us apply its real meaning to our own lives.

WHEN WOULD YOU USE THEM?

Use handbooks and commentaries when you want to look deeper into the background or meaning of a passage.

HOW DO YOU USE THEM?

Handbooks have introductory material and comments on books of the Bible listed in the order they're arranged in the Bible. For commentaries, simply go to the chapter and verse you're looking for. Commentaries are arranged in the same order the Bible is.

In the Olden Days

Preparation: You'll need one or two costume props relevant to the late 1500s: household implements such as wooden spoons; scrub boards (instead of washing machines); candles or paraffin lamps; cotton or woolen clothes instead of jeans, polyester, or silk; chalk, pencils, and quill pens. Write on a flip chart or chalkboard the list of things someone in 1599 would never have seen or heard about. Have your room lit by paraffin lamps and candles instead of electricity. Have a variety of craft supplies available.

Say: **Sometimes, we don't realize how much we know. Imagine that you woke up and found yourself living in 1599. The people are talking a different language. They've never heard of electricity, washable markers, public schools, TV, radio, football, North America, cars, ovens, bicycles, or democracy. What else wouldn't they know about?** Let the children make suggestions to add to your list. Ask:

● **How could you help these people of 1599 understand what our lives are like?**

Say: **Choose one of the things on our list, and make a "tool" to help you explain it to someone living four hundred years ago. You can make a picture, a model, or write about it—maybe even all three!** After children have made their "tools," say: **There are many things someone living in 1599 would know how to do** that we wouldn't: make their own candles, soap, butter, cloth, mattresses, and beds. And they could cook all their food over an open fire. They understood some things that are not common knowledge today.

It's the same with the people in Bible days. They had knowledge to help them live in their world that most of us no longer need today. Bible handbooks and commentaries are like the tools you made. They help us understand life in Bible times. Knowing that can help us understand why the Bible says certain things in the way it does.

Get Some Culture

Preparation: Write a question about a cultural norm or tradition (write one question per blank paper, and have one paper per group):
- When would you give someone one of your sandals?
- Why would you build a pile of stones?
- Why would you wash a visitor's feet before dinner?
- Why would you put an altar on top of a hill?
- Why would you bring doves or a lamb to church?

Give each group a paper. Say: **Each of these were normal, everyday things to the people in the Bible. In your groups, see if you can come up with an explanation for these traditions. When all of you have had a chance to come up with an idea, you'll pantomime your "tradition" to the class. Have fun thinking of solutions. If you don't know what the real answer to your question is, make up something fun. Then we'll talk about the answers found in a Bible handbook or commentary.**

After each group has acted out its idea, tell kids the correct answers:
- Giving a sandal sealed a business deal. Today, it would be like putting your signature on a contract (Ruth 4).
- Israelites often piled stones as a sign that something important had happened. When they saw the pile, they told their children about the event (Joshua 4).
- Hosts washed visitor's feet because everyone wore sandals and the roads were messy (John 13).
- Altars were built on top of hills because high places were strategic in controlling the land. People put altars there as a sign that the gods or God controlled the land (throughout Kings).
- Doves or lambs were brought to church (the temple) to be sacrificed to God. They were an offering for sins or as thanks for God's provision (Leviticus 1-7).

Say: **Bible tools help explain these strange things to us so we understand them. Otherwise some of the stories in the Bible wouldn't make sense to us. Knowing about them helps us understand more about the people who lived in those days and helps us get more out of the stories.**

Bible Tools Inserts

Preparation: Photocopy the "Bible Tools" handout provided on page 57 (one per child).

Say: **We've learned about a lot of different study tools and how they help us learn more about the Bible. Here is a page you can keep in your Bible to help you remember when to use the different tools.**

BIBLE TOOLS

Use This Tool   When You Need...

TOPICAL INDEX . . . . When you want to study a topic, go to this tool. It lists topics alphabetically, giving the main verses and passages so you can look them up and more easily study the topic.

BIBLE DICTIONARY . . . . . . When you're not sure what a word you find in the Bible means, what a nation or person was like, or what the Bible says about a doctrine or belief, this is your tool. Just look up the word alphabetically.

CONCORDANCE . . . . Use this tool when you know a word from a verse but can't find it, or when you want to know which passages contain a certain word. Look up the word alphabetically, and read through the phrases until you find the right one, or study the Scriptures that contain the word to get the full picture.

BIBLE ATLAS/MAPS . . . . Use these tools to locate the places you're reading about, to see how far apart the towns are, or where people went on their journeys. Look up the place names in the index.

**HANDBOOK AND
COMMENTARY** . . . . Use these tools whenever you want to dig deeper into what the Bible means. They explain what the Hebrew and Greek words mean and show how the culture and background of the time helps us better understand the Bible. Look up the chapter and verse you want to know more about.

Chapter Four

OVERCOMING OBSTACLES TO UNDERSTANDING

Dennis R. McLaughlin

Understanding is the critical factor in both teaching and learning the Bible. While Bible memorization is impressive, without understanding, it does little to help children in their relationship with God. So what are some of the things that hinder children's understanding of the Bible, and what can we do to help them?

One of the primary stumbling blocks in understanding the Bible is the misconception that it's presented in chronological order. We need to acknowledge that our Western culture teaches us to think in a linear fashion, often chronologically. Kids are taught to say their "ABCs" in order and are admonished for getting them out of sequence. The same is true when they learn to count. Kids even learn the books of the Bible in order. As a result, they expect the events of the Bible to be in order as well. Certain books do follow a true time line, but others do not. An effective Bible teacher will recognize this as a potential obstacle and will help students recognize it as well.

Another potentially confusing thing for children is the abundance of translations available. While an easy-to-understand translation can be the best tool to foster a child's daily Bible reading, it may be difficult to understand how the same verse can be memorized with different words (too often, one translation leading to a candy bar, the other leading to subtle disapproval because the words "aren't right"!).

Children also often have difficulty with anything they perceive as incongruity in a story. For example, when they hear about the feeding of the five thousand from different Gospels, they wonder which one is true. And if one is true, then the others must be false, and if part of the Bible is false, then it could all be false…and on goes the circle of childlike reasoning. Instead, you can challenge your students to higher-level thinking and strengthen their faith at the same time.

Finally, we'll look at some patterns and conditions for learning that will make your classroom the most Bible-friendly place it can be. For children to make effective Christian decisions on a daily basis, they must both know and understand God's Word. Our primary objective as Christian educators must be to reinforce our students' understanding of the Scriptures in every way we can. Use these tools to get you started, and apply the principles with different passages as the Holy Spirit leads you.

BIBLE CHRONOLOGY

Use the life and art of King David to help kids understand the ordering system of the Bible.

One of the first Bible study principles a child learns is to find the Psalms by opening his or her Bible to the middle. The observant child will notice that many of the Psalms are written by King David. Unfortunately, eight books earlier David died and was buried (1 Kings 2:1-10).

The predominantly chronological section of the Old Testament actually ends at the conclusion of the book of Nehemiah. If a child is seeking to understand the Bible as though it were written in historical or chronological order, the best we can expect is total confusion, because there are still twenty-three more books in the Old Testament.

Putting Things in Order

Have children line up in order by height. Be sure to let them complete the task with as little help from you as possible. The most effective way for children to learn is through their own experiences.

After they have lined up, ask: **If you believe you are in the correct order, raise your hand.**

Say: **Next, line up in order of your hair shades, beginning with those who have the darkest hair and ending with those who have the lightest.**

Once they have accomplished this, say: **If you believe you are in the correct order, raise your hand.**

When they respond in the affirmative, ask: **How can you be in order now, when you were in order a while ago?** They will begin to understand that there is more than one kind of order.

Finally, have them line up according to their birthdays. Again, when they are in line, ask: **How do you know you are in order?**

Say: **There are many different kinds of order. When we line up in order of** when we were born, what happens to the order of how tall we are?

Ask: **What are some other ways you can line up and still be in order?** Allow them time to respond, and then have the students line up using some of their own ordering patterns.

Say: **Bible order is similar. Bible stories are not always in order by dates, called chronological order (when things happen). Let me show you what I mean. Turn to Psalm 3, look at the very beginning, and see who wrote it.** *(David wrote it.)*

Now turn your Bibles to 1 Kings 2:10, and read it.

Ask: **What happened?** *(David was buried.)* **How could David have died and still have written Psalm 3 eight books later?** By now kids should recognize that much of the Bible is not in order of when things actually happened. Point out that the book of Psalms is one of the books of Poetry, not of History. (See details in Chapter Two.)

For another comparison, use 1 Chronicles 14:8. This passage is two books after the 1 Kings passage and again speaks of David when he is alive and well. Reading Kings and Chronicles is like reading history books by two different authors—some of the information reported is the same, yet specific details may vary.

It's About Time

While there are many different ways to study the Bible, studying it by theme or topic can often confuse young students if they haven't learned the basic order of biblical events.

To help your students gain an overall perspective of biblical events, it's helpful to link Bible times to kid-relevant world history events. While the comparison of the following time line is not exact year for year, it is based on a proximate time frame.

The best way to employ a simple chronology tool like this is to have your students develop it using newsprint, markers, crayons, or paint. Challenge them to do their own research and to be creative in their presentation, making a mural or collage that can be added to as they learn more. Post the chronology line in a prominent place so kids can refer to it often.

BIBLE CHRONOLOGY LINE

Bible Events	World Events
Creation	first people on earth
Noah builds the ark	dogs first used as pets
Tower of Babel built	pyramids built in Egypt
Abraham born	cats first used as pets
Isaac born	watermelon first cultivated
Jacob born	ice cream invented
Moses born	sundials used to tell time
Ten Commandments given	first clock used in Egypt
God's people cross into promised land	modern writing developed
Saul becomes first king	multiplication first used
David becomes king	modern brick making developed
Solomon becomes king	wearing jewelry becomes popular
Jonah runs from God	Olympic games first held
God's people taken into captivity	horse racing begins
Daniel in the lion's den	first coins used
God's people released from captivity	public libraries first open
Esther risks life to save people	paved roads become common
Jesus born	sumo wrestling begins in Japan
Paul begins preaching	first paintings on canvas

Chronology Calendar

Another effective tool in teaching the events of the Bible is to use a chronology calendar. (See "Chronology Calendar" handout on p. 63.) This particular example is applied to a specific book rather then the whole Bible. Chronology calendars can be applied to any book in the Bible. You can use them to study the life of a particular character, the details of a particular event, or the chronology of a whole book.

To most effectively use this calendar, send it home with students. Before you do, encourage them to set aside time each day to read and think about the particular Bible passage assigned. This activity works especially well with students who can read. For the younger ones, consider asking parents to help.

To make using this calendar especially fun, prepare two copies of page 63. Then "white-out" the print on one of the copies. Make one copy of the "Chronology Calendar" and one copy of the blank calendar for each child. Cut each day of the blank calendar so that it can be lifted (like a flap). Place a strip of self-adhesive magnetic tape at the top and bottom of the back of each of these sheets. Glue a small wrapped candy to each of the days of the printed "Chronology Calendar," and then glue the unprinted calendar on top of the printed calendar, so that kids can hang them on their refrigerators and open one day at a time to get the Bible message and the treat.

TRANSLATION RELATION

There are many wonderful translations of the Bible available to your students. In fact, during any given class session, your students may bring several different ones to class. When someone reads aloud from a translation that doesn't correspond word for word to the version a particular child is following along in, it can be confusing, especially in light of wanting kids to understand that the Bible is inspired by God. To illustrate some of the reasons for differences in Bible translations, and to help your students better understand the reasons behind these differences, try using this parallel activity.

The Translation Shuffle

Preparation: You'll need index cards, pens or pencils, and a copy of the "Bible Translations" handout on page 65.

Give each student an index card and a pen or pencil. Next, have the students watch you as you walk back and forth in front of the class. As you do, say: **Write**

Chronology Calendar

				1	2	3
				Jesus' birth announced—Luke 1:26-38	John the Baptist born—Luke 1:57-61	Jesus born—Luke 2:1-7
4	5	6	7	8	9	10
Twelve-year-old Jesus visits temple—Luke 2:41-50	Jesus grows up—Luke 2:51-52	Jesus baptized by John—Luke 3:21-23	Jesus tempted in desert—Luke 4:1-13	Jesus begins preaching—Luke 4:42-44	Jesus calls disciples—Luke 5:1-11	Jesus heals a paralyzed man—Luke 5:17-26
11	12	13	14	15	16	17
Jesus calms the sea—Luke 8:22-25	Jesus sends disciples to teach—Luke 9:1-6	John the Baptist killed—Luke 9:7-9	Jesus feeds five thousand—Luke 9:10-17	Jesus with Elijah and Moses—Luke 9:28-36	Jesus tells about the Good Samaritan—Luke 10:25-37	Jesus teaches the Lord's prayer—Luke 11:1-13
18	19	20	21	22	23	24
Jesus heals ten lepers—Luke 17:12-19	Jesus blesses the children—Luke 18:15-17	Jesus heals blind beggar—Luke 18:35-42	Jesus finds Zacchaeus in the tree—Luke 19:1-10	Jesus enters city on a donkey—Luke 19:28-44	Jesus' last supper with disciples—Luke 22:17-20	Jesus prays in the garden—Luke 22:39-46
25	26	27	28	29	30	31
Jesus betrayed and arrested—Luke 22:47-53	Peter denies Jesus—Luke 22:54-62	Jesus crucified—Luke 23:26-43	Jesus buried—Luke 23:50-55	Women find empty tomb—Luke 24:1-11	Jesus appears to disciples—Luke 24:36-49	Jesus taken to heaven—Luke 24:50-53

as many words on your cards as you can think of to describe what I'm doing right now. Continue to pace for another minute, slightly varying your speed and style of movement.

Next, have all kids share their words to see how many different ones they came up with to describe your pacing movement. Kids may only be able to list simple words such as "walking" or "stepping," or they may take off with words like "sauntering," "ambling," or "circumnavigating"!

Say: **We were able to come up with several different words to describe what I was doing.** Ask:

● **What would you think if someone said I was "crawling"?**

● **Why were we able to use different words to accurately describe the same movement?**

Say: **What we have discovered is that sometimes a change in words changes the meaning in a tiny way, and sometimes it changes it in a big way. "Crawling" and "walking" both describe a movement, but there's a big difference. "Walking" and "stepping" both describe a movement, but the difference is slight. That is an important point for us to keep in mind as we think about different translations of the Bible. There are often many different ways to describe something. Let's look at an example.**

Give each student a copy of the "Bible Translations" handout on page 65. Have them spend a few minutes comparing the different versions. After two or three minutes, divide them into small groups of three or four participants, and have the groups discuss the following questions:

● **What are some of the differences between the different translations?**

● **Which one is easiest for you to understand?**

● **Why might the people who translate the Bible use different words to describe the same thing?**

Say: **The Bible was originally written in the Hebrew and Greek languages. Hebrew and Greek both have many words that mean close to the same thing, in the same way that "walking" and "stepping" mean close to the same thing. The different translations you looked at all take the words from the original languages and translate them as closely to an English word or thought as possible. There are many complicated rules for translating from one language to another. The last verse on your work sheet is from a paraphrase of the Bible. That means that the author tried to retell the message of the verse in a way that people could best understand it today, without using all the rules of translators.**

Have kids attempt to write their own paraphrases of the verse on the backs of their handouts. Remind them that they can't make it say *anything* they want it to, but they can restate the author's idea in their own way. Let the group share their paraphrases.

BIBLE TRANSLATIONS
(Psalm 100:1-2)

NEW INTERNATIONAL VERSION:
"Shout for joy to the Lord, all the earth. Serve the Lord with gladness; come before him with joyful songs."

KING JAMES VERSION:
"Make a joyful noise unto the Lord, all ye lands. Serve the Lord with gladness: come before his presence with singing."

NEW REVISED STANDARD VERSION:
"Make a joyful noise to the Lord, all the earth. Worship the Lord with gladness; come into his presence with singing."

NEW CENTURY VERSION:
"Shout to the Lord, all the earth. Serve the Lord with joy; come before him with singing."

THE MESSAGE (paraphrase)
"On your feet now—applaud God! Bring a gift of laughter, sing yourselves in his presence."

Paraphrase Patterns

Have kids form groups of three to four, and give each group a piece of paper and a pen or pencil. Read aloud the following story to the kids:

The Old Stone Archway

When Jack was a small boy, every Saturday morning he would walk with his grandfather to the bakery. The old brick road they traveled was narrow and shaded by many trees. There was scarcely anyone else out at that time of morning. After what always seemed to Jack to be a long walk, they would pass beneath an old stone archway that served as a bridge over the road. It was then that he would know they were near their journey's end.

One morning, just as they were walking under the archway, Jack noticed a small dead rabbit beside the road. He stopped for a moment to look at it. His grandfather, noticing the young boy standing compassionately over the rabbit, walked to his side and put his arm around him.

"It's so small, Grandpa. Why did it live such a short life?" asked the young boy.

Jack's grandfather paused for a moment and then answered, "In many ways Jack, our lives, too, will be short like this young rabbit's. But we must not labor too long with these earthly matters, instead we must think of spending an eternity with God."

"But how long shall I live, Grandpa, and how long is eternity?"

"Look up at that old archway, my young Jack. Each time we journey along this road, we walk beneath its shadow. Think about how quickly we pass beneath it. Your life, Jack, is much like walking beneath the archway. God's eternity is like the rest of the journey. Our lives are short, and we must make the best of them. But God's eternity is much greater. And that, Jack, is where our hearts and minds must be focused."

Next, instruct each group to retell the story in its own words and write it down. After about ten or fifteen minutes, have a representative from each group read aloud its story.

Afterward ask:

- **How are the stories from each group different?**
- **How are they the same?**
- **What if one group had written a story about a boy named Joel who found a bird?**

Say: **When we retell a story, that's called a paraphrase. We take the ideas and put them into our own words, but we can't change the details. Often, we consider the words our audience knows and choose those words instead of more complicated ones, so that it will be easy for our audience to read and understand.** Ask:

- **What do you think are some of the main things a person who is paraphrasing should be careful about?**

- How can other people's paraphrases help you?
- How could it help you to paraphrase a Bible verse yourself?

Encourage kids to use this technique, but to remember that when they restate a Bible verse, they must be careful that the main message stays the same. Putting a verse into their own words can be a very effective way to help them remember and apply the principle of the verse.

UNDERSTANDING INCONGRUITIES

Remembering Home

Preparation: You'll need paper, pencils, newsprint, markers, and tape.

The writers of the Bible were inspired by God and carefully directed by him. A fun way to explore this concept is to have students write a simple description of their own homes.

Afterward, ask them to share what they have written. Point out that few of them, if any, wrote about their homes in the order of walking through it from the front door to the back door. So in a way, their descriptions were out of order, or at least not in chronological order.

Ask: **Why did you choose to write about your homes as you did? Why might those who wrote the Bible have chosen different ways to report events?**

Next, have your students form four groups. Give each group a piece of newsprint and a marker. Assign each group one of the following passages: Matthew 14:13-21; Mark 6:30-44; Luke 9:10-17; and John 6:1-15.

Say: **Each group has been assigned the story of when Jesus fed five thousand people. But each passage was written by a different person. Each group should carefully read their passage and then record the order of events on your newsprint. After approximately ten minutes, we will come back together and each group will make a report.**

After the groups have finished, tape the reports on a front wall next to one another. Have a representative from each group come up and talk about the order of events in the passage his or her group was assigned. After each report has been given, lead a short discussion by asking:

- **How do each of these reports differ?**
- **In what ways are they the same?**
- **Why is each report a little different, even though it describes the same event?**
- **Do you believe that any of the reports are wrong? Explain your answer.**

Observing and Reporting

Children have a natural curiosity and may be searching for a reason why sometimes there are different accounts of the same story. To help them better understand this, try this activity.

Take kids out to the parking lot. Pick out one parked vehicle, and say: **Spend two or three minutes observing this vehicle very carefully. Walk around it, and notice details that are important to you. When we get back inside, I'm going to ask you each to write or dictate a description of your observations.**

Once back inside, give each student a pencil and a sheet of paper. Have each one write a description of the car. Younger children can dictate their descriptions so that you or an older buddy can write them. When they have finished, ask them to read their descriptions. Afterward, say: **I noticed that each of you observed and wrote a little differently about the car, and definitely in a different order.**

Ask: **Why were your reports different when all of you were reporting on the same car?**

Say: **While each of your descriptions were correct, each one of you saw the vehicle a little differently. Some of you thought that the color was the most important thing. Others thought the shape and type of vehicle was most important. The Bible is much the same. After God revealed his plan, he needed a way to pass it on from generation to generation. So God gave people like Moses, Jeremiah, Luke, Mark, Matthew, Paul, and Peter the responsibility to write it. When you read through the Bible books about Jesus' life, it may appear that some of the stories in Matthew are not in the same order as they are in Luke. Keep in mind that the order of what happened in Jesus' life was not always the most important thing for some of the writers.** Ask:

● **How might each writer's report have been like the report each of us wrote about the vehicle we observed?**

● **How would your report have been different if you were speaking to someone who had never even seen a vehicle before?**

● **In the same way, why might Matthew, Mark, Luke, and John have used different ways to write about Jesus depending on who they were speaking to?**

Be sure to point out that there is a difference between students writing a report about something and those who were inspired by God to write the Bible. God knew the audience of each book even better than the writer did, and God chose each writer for his own reasons and purposes.

CREATING A BIBLE-FRIENDLY FOCUS

To make your classroom not only Bible rich, but also Bible friendly, it's important to know a little bit about how learning happens. While volumes have been written on learning theory, here are just a few concepts to consider as you help kids know, use, and understand their Bibles.

Kids have a God-given need to search for meaning—to make sense of what they encounter. They (and you!) do this by association and patterning. In short, that means that every new piece of information needs to be linked to something else they already know. Because every learner is different, each must find his or her own unique link to new information, and each must make the link in his or her own way. New "stuff" becomes deeply ingrained largely because of a link to something kids really care about, because it's emotionally charged by relationship, humor, or significance to their lives.

Learning is inhibited when there is no relationship, poor modeling, high stress (such as in competition, which may lead to high levels of performance, but low levels of retention), or little opportunity to search for association or to practice real life application.

So, to be Bible friendly, we must create an environment where we model dependence on God's Word as the authority for every issue kids face. We must refer to it often as one would refer to the advice of a loving friend, not as to the rod of a severe taskmaster. We must offer kids the opportunity to think about and experience God's Word through their own learning styles, intelligences, and senses and to use it as a filter for their own life experiences.

We must also give them opportunities to share what is really happening in their lives, and interact with them in a way that helps them make real-life applications of God's Word. Without opportunity to explore and work out what the Christian life looks like in the company of other believers, children are limited to knowledge of the Bible without real understanding. Kids really do internalize concepts that are modeled for them based on the strength of the relationship to the model. In other words, kids become like the people they hang around! Make sure your classroom gives them the opportunity to "hang around" others who are in the process of making sound, Bible-based choices about their lives.

The remainder of this book is dedicated to providing specific suggestions for maximizing kids' opportunities to drink in God's Word.

CREATING ASSOCIATIONS

Mnemonics are a great device for helping kids create associations, or learning links. Simply put, mnemonics are images that help a person remember something. Our minds are structured in a way that allows us to make strong mnemonic links between things we want to remember and cues we use for their recall. These cues can take the form of pictures, words, stories, sounds, or movements. Each time a child colors or designs a picture in a meaningful way, especially if he or she uses symbols, it becomes a pictorial mnemonic or picture-memory cue. If you encourage children to be creative, they will come up with some very fun and effective symbols and pictures to help them remember biblical content, so they can extend the concepts to lifelong application.

Animal Picture Mnemonics

A fun activity is to divide your class into groups and assign each group one or two different books of the Bible. Challenge them to think of an animal that represents each book they have been assigned and then draw a picture of that animal. Then let each group share with the others what animal it chose to represent its assigned book and why. Afterward, call for volunteers to recall all the books and animals that have been presented.

A variation is to challenge each group to come up with a different animal to represent each book of the Bible. The animal link may be based on events in the book (such as camels for Genesis and lions for Daniel), or may be based on the sound of the name of the book (such as zebra for Zephaniah).

This device can also be used to remember in order the events of a story or book. Challenge kids to form a circus parade of animals linked together by their tails.

Lots of Lists

There are many lists of things in the Bible we'd like kids to remember so they can use the concepts later.

Here are two types of mnemonics for helping kids remember the fruit of the Spirit found in Galatians 5:22-23. The character traits to be remembered are

Love
Joy
Peace
Patience
Kindness
Goodness
Faithfulness
Gentleness
Self-control

Using the first letter of each word we can create a word-story mnemonic such as *Little Johnny Paraded Past Kentucky Going Fast, Going Slow*. Remember that children recall best when their associations are specific to their own experience, so allowing children to create word-story mnemonics of their own is even more effective.

The sample sentence is easy for children to remember, especially after they have said it several times and even acted it out with a paper outline of the state of Kentucky. After they commit the simple story to memory, it will be easy for them to recall the fruit of the Spirit by associating the first letters.

This works because instead of remembering isolated words, kids can remember a single "chunked" thought. The strategy of chunking helps us to remember a group of items because it is linked to a single thought, much as we "chunk" a telephone number.

The second option is to have kids create their own picture mnemonic, selecting nine different fruits and naming each of them one of the fruits of the Spirit. They can take this a step beyond visualization by actually drawing out the fruits and labeling them. These can be recalled as a bowl of fruit, a fruit salad, a fruit sculpture, or even a fruit square dance! Encourage kids to develop memorable pictures in their own minds, with a reason each fruit reminds them of a particular fruit of the Spirit.

Content Counts

Let's look at an example of a rhyming word mnemonic and how we can apply it to an overview of the book of Genesis.

You might choose the following divisions for an overview:

Creation, Fall, Flood, Abraham, Isaac, Jacob, Joseph

To create a rhyming word story mnemonic, you might come up with the following:

> Creation, Fall,
> Flood destroyed it all,
> Abraham, Isaac,
> Jacob, Joe
> God's people chosen
> Long ago.

It's not so important that every word is spoken exactly as you want the list memorized, but that the rhyme captures the links to the memory in sequence.

To create a rhyming word mnemonic for an overview of Jonah, you could use the following divisions:

Disobedience, Ship experience, Fish experience, Prayer experience, Dry land experience, Obedience

To commit these chronological occurrences to memory, you might come up with the following:

> Disobey, float away,
> Swallowed by a fish,
> Lots of prayer, spit out there,
> Obey as God wished.

Landmark Learning

Another way in which you can use the mnemonic concept is by employing the use of landmarks or a simple journey. Suppose you wanted the kids to have an overview of the life of Jesus. You might list the events of his life in this way: birth, baptism, preached Sermon on the Mount, healed many people, raised Lazarus from the dead, crucified, resurrected, and ascended to heaven.

To help kids remember these distinctions, you could map out a simple journey for them using various landmarks around the church. When you are ready to begin, say: **We are going to go on a journey to learn about the life of Jesus. Each place I will take you will help you remember the story. Work on remembering the order in which we take our journey. In each place, I will ask you how it relates to the life of Jesus.**

Lead the kids to the nursery, and ask: **What does this room have to do with remembering the story of Jesus?** *(It reminds us of his birth.)*

Lead them to where your church baptizes people, and ask: **What does this have to do with remembering Jesus' life?** *(It reminds us of his baptism.)*

Next, take them to the place your pastor preaches from, and ask: **What does this place have to do with the life of Jesus?** *(He preached the Sermon on the Mount.)*

Take them to where the church's first-aid kit is kept, show it to them, and ask: **What does this have to do with the life of Jesus?** *(He healed many people.)*

Lead them to a dark closet, open the door, and ask: **What does this have to do with remembering the life of Jesus?** *(He raised Lazarus from the tomb.* While kids may at first have difficulty making this connection, even if you help them, they won't soon forget the imagery.)

Lead them to a cross somewhere in the church, and ask: **What does this have to do with Jesus' life?** *(He was crucified.)*

Finally, lead them outside, have them look into the sky, and ask: **What does this have to do with Jesus' life?** *(He was resurrected and ascended to heaven.)*

When you have completed your journey, have kids recall each location in its proper order and what it had to do with Jesus' life.

The journeys you can take are as endless as your imagination. A variation you might want to consider on this mnemonic is to set up learning centers, or tables, with a different activity at each one that represents an idea you want kids to remember.

The use of mnemonics can be endless. Story mnemonics are particularly effective for dominant learning styles that are language-based (such as linguistic and interpersonal intelligences), picture mnemonics are great for visual learners, and rhyme mnemonics are effective for auditory learners and musical intelligences. Landmark mnemonics connect kinesthetic or body-smart learners, as well as kids who seem to learn through a naturalistic intelligence—especially when the landmarks are outdoor ones. (See Appendix for more on multiple intelligences.) Let your kids make up mnemonics as a way of creatively interacting with the Bible. The more you stimulate your kids' creativity, the more they will connect to, remember, and apply the biblical principles God gave to make their lives abundant!

As you put these and other learning tools to use, be sure to rely on the imagination of the kids, and as you stimulate them to use their God-given creativity, remember—they are wonderfully made (Psalm 139:14).

Chapter Five

THE BIBLE COMES ALIVE

LaDona L. Hein and Janet Colsher Teitsort

PREREADING ACTIVITIES

Discovery of the special qualities of God's Word can begin long before children are able to read it. We can encourage young children to develop an emotional bond to the Bible by the special way we treat it and refer to it. Use these ideas with children as young as two to build lifelong intimacy with this gift of God's love.

The Bible Deserves a Special Place

Here are some things you can do to help children understand that the Bible is different from any other book, and belongs not on a shelf, but in our hearts.

- Put the Bible in a lined basket so it can easily be carried.
- Put the Bible in a small suitcase or cosmetic bag to emphasize that the Bible is to take with us wherever we go.
- Find a special drawer or shelf where the Bible can stay open instead of shelved as other books are.
- Put a new Bible or Bible storybook in a gift-wrapped box, and let children open it. Talk about how the Bible is a special gift, not just for one of us but for all of us. Spark interest in an old Bible or Bible storybook by wrapping a pretty ribbon and bow around it.
- Let children build a Bible bookstand from blocks. Because the Bible is special, leave the stand set up until the next session, instead of putting the blocks away at the end of class "like we always do."
- Make a treasure chest out of a foam ice chest. Spray paint it gold, add jewels, and then put the Bible inside, because the Bible is a great treasure.
- Use a map as a table cover. Put the Bible on top of it, and talk about how the Bible gives us directions for our lives.

● Put the Bible in the center of a bowl filled with real or plastic fruit. Talk about how the Bible gives us healthy fuel for our spiritual lives just as fruit gives our bodies healthy fuel to move and grow. You could also set the Bible in the middle of a canned-food display to make the same connection.

● Make super simple take-home carriers to give to children for a special occasion. Cut a piece of felt six inches longer than a child's open Bible and about one-half inch wider. Three inches from the edge, stitch ribbon about eight inches in length to each short side of the felt; then fold the felt away from the ribbon, forming a three-inch flap on each side. Glue the edges with fabric glue, or stitch them so that you can insert the Bible cover in the flaps. Tie the ribbons to form a handle. Use fabric paint to write kids' names on the covers. Kids can use stickers to decorate the felt again and again.

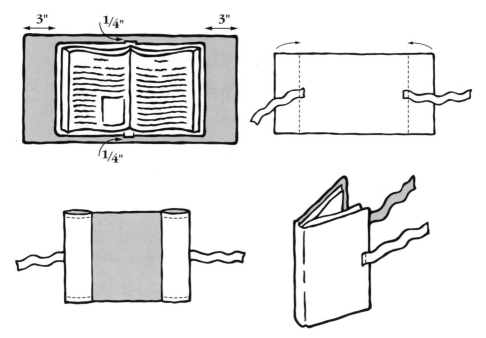

● Let kids make their own special boxes to keep their Bibles in at home.

Materials Needed
- ☐ shoe boxes, gift boxes, or cereal boxes
- ☐ assorted pieces of fabric or wrapping paper
- ☐ scissors, glue, pencils, fabric pen, wooden clothespins
- ☐ assorted stickers, ribbon, buttons, and rickrack
- ☐ pictures of the children

Directions

Let children choose their own boxes. It is important for children to make their own choices so they feel that this project is really theirs. Once children choose their boxes, allow each child to choose materials to cover the box. Apply glue to the back of the covering, and use wooden clothespins to hold it in place while it dries.

Children may glue their pictures on the lids. They may finish their boxes with various decorations to make each box uniquely personalized.

Make a Divider Between the Old and New Testament

Materials Needed
- ☐ 5x7-inch blank index cards
- ☐ clear self-adhesive plastic (or laminating film)
- ☐ parchment or other antique-looking paper, cut into 5x7-inch pieces
- ☐ stickers or pictures of Jesus
- ☐ glue sticks

Directions

Show children the index cards and the antique-looking paper. Talk about which paper looks old and which looks new. Ask:

● **How do you know the difference between something that is old and something that is new?**

● **What are some new things that are good?**

● **What are some old things that are good?**

Say: **Our Bibles have a part we call the Old Testament and a part we call the New Testament. Both parts are good. The new part tells us about Jesus and the people who lived after him, and the old part tells us about the people who lived before Jesus. We're going to make a card to go inside our Bibles that shows us where the Old Testament ends and where the New Testament begins.**

First have children glue the old-looking paper to the index cards. Then have them turn the index cards over and attach the picture of Jesus to the new-looking side. Help children cover their cards with the self-adhesive plastic or laminating film.

Help children locate the correct place to insert the cards in their own Bibles. Suggest to parents that they might want to apply glue to the edge of both sides of the card and push it down between the appropriate pages so the card doesn't come out.

Use this card frequently during lessons, helping children identify whether the Bible story you are focusing on happened *before* Jesus was born (Old Testament) or *after* (New Testament). You may also have children identify whether they would find the story in the *front* (Old Testament) or the *back* (New Testament) of their Bibles.

Story Sort

Materials Needed
- ☐ Bible character pictures from previous lessons
- ☐ a Bible
- ☐ a brown paper bag
- ☐ clean, fresh-looking butcher paper

Directions

Tear apart the brown bag, and wad it into a tight ball; then open it, and smooth it out so that it looks like old paper. Lay this beside the clean, fresh-looking piece of paper.

Hold up a character picture, and briefly recount the story (better yet, say the character's name, and let the kids recount the story). Ask:

- **Did this story happen before or after Jesus was born?**
- **Is this story part of the Old Testament or the New Testament?**

Allow kids to take turns placing the character on the appropriate piece of paper. You may choose to mount the pictures on the paper and hang these posters in your classroom so that as you learn new Bible stories, kids can place the characters appropriately.

Sing a Song of Scripture

Use the following songs to help children connect to the Bible.

WHERE'S THE BIBLE? (Tune: "Where is Thumbkin?")

Place the Bible in a different visible location each time you sing this song.

Where's the Bible? *(Hold both hands palms up.)*
Where's the Bible?
There it is. *(Point to the Bible.)*
There it is.
It's about my special friend,
It's about my special friend.
I love him. *(Hug self; then point up.)*
I love him.

PAGE BY PAGE (Tune: "Itsy Bitsy Spider")

I turn the pages carefully and learn about God's love. *(Pantomime turning pages.)*
I turn the pages carefully and learn about God's love.
The Bible is a special book sent from God above *(make a book shape with hands together),*
So I turn the pages carefully and learn about God's love.

LOTS OF STORIES (Tune: "London Bridge")

Sing this song through several times, pausing between each repetition to let children tell about stories they remember from the Bible, or have a children's picture Bible close at hand, and let a child open it at random and show the picture to his or her classmates. Then each person can tell what he or she knows about that story, like the name of the characters and what happened to them.

I am learning lots of stories,
Lots of stories,
Lots of stories.
I am learning lots of stories,
From the Bible.

THE BIBLE, MY FRIEND (Tune: "Farmer in the Dell")

Jumping up and down *(children stand and jump),*
Turning all around *(children turn around),*
The Bible is my helper *(children clap),*
The Bible is my friend. *(Children sit down.)*

I LOVE HEAR'N ABOUT THE BIBLE (Tune: "Jesus Loves the Little Children")

I love hear'n about the Bible.
Love to learn about my Lord,
'Bout how Jesus came to earth,
'Bout how much to God I'm worth!
I love hear'n about the Bible, God's Word.

OH, HOW I LOVE GOD'S WORD (Tune: "Oh, How I Love Jesus")

Make sure each child has a Bible to hug as they sing this song!

Oh, how I love God's Word.
Oh, how I love God's Word.
Oh, how I love God's Word,
The Bible God gave to me.

IF YOU LOVE GOD'S WORD (Tune: "If You're Happy and You Know It")

Substitute "stomp your feet," "blow a kiss," "squat down," or any other motions you can think of for "clap your hands"!

If you love God's Word, clap your hands.
If you love God's Word, clap your hands.
If you love God's Word more than anything you've heard,
If you love God's Word, clap your hands!

Making Listening Time Special

Let kids create a special mat only they can sit on as they listen to stories from the Bible.

Materials Needed
☐ a light-colored dish towel or handkerchief for each child
☐ fabric crayons
☐ an iron

Directions

Let each child color one or more Bible pictures (or any other design) with the fabric crayons. Heat the iron in a safe area. If you use the iron around the children, make sure you observe every safety precaution. Lay one towel at a time on a flat surface, place a Bible picture upside down on the towel, and lay the hot iron over the top to transfer the crayon from the paper to the towel. (Hint: Press the iron down flat without rotating it. If the picture is larger than the surface of the iron, press it down flat in sections.) Kids will be delighted with their personalized story mats. If you lose some of the facial features in the transfer process, consider attaching wiggly eyes and felt facial features with fabric glue.

The Book for Me

Glue a small unbreakable mirror inside the front cover of your (or each child's) Bible. Before you read your story, say: **Today I have a story from the Bible for a special person. Would you like to know who this story is for?**

Let each child come up and open the Bible and look into the mirror. Watch their faces as they realize the story is for them! You can't do this activity too often with little ones (and it's a great reminder for adults, too!)

Sing the song "The B-I-B-L-E" together before your story time.

Food for Thought

Make these sweet Bible snacks for children to eat as they listen to a story.

Materials Needed
- graham crackers or chocolate graham crackers (two per child)
- peanut butter or marshmallow cream
- red string licorice (one per child)
- plastic knives
- napkins

Spread a thick layer of peanut butter or marshmallow cream on half of the graham cracker squares, or allow the children to do this. Place a piece of licorice at the top left corner of the cracker to look like a ribbon bookmark. Lay a second cracker over the top. Say: **This might look like the Bible. Where is the cover? Where are the pages?**

The Bible tells us that God's Word is sweet. We'll eat these sweet little Bibles to remind us how good it is to have the Bible.

Bible Treasure Keepers

God knows and cares about everything that's important to kids. Kids love to collect all kinds of treasures, from bottle caps to butterfly wings and bird feathers. Encourage kids to let God be part of their treasure hunting by making these treasure keepers to place inside their Bibles, or with permission from parents, glue them onto the back covers of their Bibles so they can hold "stuff" that's not flat.

Materials Needed
- 5x7-inch envelopes (preferably with string closures rather than brad closures, but either will work)
- treasure or gem stickers, and letter stickers (optional)

Have kids decorate their envelopes with stickers. Then have them discuss some treasures they might find during a day. Encourage them to place those little treasures inside their envelopes. Then at the end of the day, they can look at their treasures and share them with God just as God shares his treasures through the Bible. They can share with God through prayers of thanksgiving for each of the special things they have collected. Be sure to enlist parents' support in this attempt to make communicating with God and spending time with the Bible part of the children's regular routine.

Picture Perfect Verses

Have your children's parents do a little investigative reporting for this special family Bible activity.

Ask parents to collect small pictures of family members and others who are significant in their children's lives. Have them search out each person's favorite Bible verse, as well, and write the reference on the back of the picture. Let parents know these photos will be used in a project and not returned in their original form.

Cut out each person's entire body from whatever picture they are part of. Cut two small holes or slits in each cutout, and thread a piece of string, ribbon, or fishing line through both holes. Locate the favorite verse indicated. Read it to the child. Point to it, and have the child mark it with a small dot or circle the verse. Now, insert the photo cutout between the pages, and bring the string or ribbon around to the spine of the Bible, and tie the ends together to secure the picture within the Bible.

When the child is looking through his or her Bible, he or she may not recognize the verse but will recognize the person who loves that verse. This helps children begin to identify early with those who they love, who also love God and his Word. Kids may ask to have the verse read to them again and again, as they associate the person with the concept that is precious to him or her.

Journaling

Help children create individual journals. "Journaling" helps us remember and share with others. Staple together about twenty pages of paper in two places. At the end of each class session, have children draw pictures about things they learned in or about God's Word. Have each child dictate a sentence as you write it on the same page with his or her drawing. Be sure to date it. Each quarter create a new journal, and send the previous one home so parents can keep a permanent record of their child's spiritual growth.

Or keep a class journal big book. You'll need a chart pad and multiple colored markers. At the top of the page, paste a picture from the Bible story of the day. Ask children what they remember or learned about the Bible story. Let each child choose a marker color, and write his or her words using that color. Be sure to read back each child's comment after you have written it. You can periodically use the journal to formally review the stories, but kids will also enjoy "reading" the book themselves when they arrive early or during a center time.

Good Things Books

Staple several sheets of paper between two pieces of poster board that are roughly the size of a child's Bible. Have children look for pictures in magazines or for photos that remind them of good things to thank God for. Have them glue the pictures inside their books. Encourage them to use these books as a prayer tool. As they look at the pictures, they can thank God for each good thing and remember that the Bible is full of good things, too.

Topical Bookmarks

Help kids create bookmarks for different topics or events in the Bible that relate to their lives. This will help kids realize that the Bible really does speak to issues that are important to them. Be sure to mark the verse the bookmark refers to. You can cut out shapes, or use die-cuts from a teacher's or scrapbook supply store. Here are some suggestions to get you started:

EVENT	SHAPE	SCRIPTURE
First snow	Snow man	Psalm 147:16
Christmas	Star	Luke 2
Birthday	Birthday cake	Jeremiah 1:5
A sunny day	Sun	Psalm 113:3
Party	Party hat	Luke 15:23
Love	Heart	John 3:16
Happiness	Happy face	Psalm 118:24
Friends	Person	Proverbs 17:17

ACTIVITIES FOR READING AND MORE!

While these activities are designed for readers, look for ways for older children to help younger ones accomplish the same goals.

Choose Your Icon

Kids who are computer savvy are familiar with the term "icon." Take advantage of this familiarity to help kids make their Bibles "high-tech" looking and functionally "high-touch."

Give each child an index card, and have them list some attributes, or characteristics, of God. They may list attributes such as loving, faithful, powerful, forgiving, and just, among others. Have them individually design small, easy-to-draw symbols that represent each attribute. Have them draw the icon next to the word on their cards. Use a concordance or topical index to locate verses that indicate each attribute, and have the children draw their icons in the margins beside them. Be careful to select a writing tool that will not bleed through the paper of their Bibles.

Have kids tape their code cards inside the cover of their Bibles. Encourage them to use their icons in their personal Bible reading whenever they encounter a verse that fits.

Personal Color Code

Give each child an index card, and identify the attributes of God as in the previous activity. But instead of designing icons, have children decide on a color each of the attributes reminds them of. When you look up the verses together, give each child a ruler and have him or her underline the verse with the selected color.

Locked In

If you encourage Scripture memory, show kids how to make a padlock icon by drawing an upside-down U on top of a square to indicate they have memorized an identified verse. It's also helpful to write a date beside the padlock. By doing this, each time a child runs across a verse they have already memorized at one point, they will be encouraged to rehearse it, providing the kind of interval reinforcement that really cements learning beyond immediate recall.

Spotlight a Verse

:—)

This is another activity that takes advantage of the technological language kids with computer skills use.

Give each child a sheet of colored office dots (the small size may work best). Have them draw a variety of emotional faces using keyboard punctuation marks (called "emoticons"). Some common ones are colon, dash, close parenthesis for a happy smile, or colon, dash, open parenthesis for a sad face. Have them repeat each emoticon on multiple stickers.

:—(

Encourage kids to use these stickers to indicate their emotional responses to a scripture verse. Have them place the dot beside the verse they read. Here are a few Scripture verses to practice with:

;—)

:—0

Isaiah 42:10-13

Mark 10:13

Romans 5:1

Encourage the kids to keep a supply of these dots tucked in their Bibles to use as they read and respond to God's Word.

Dots What I Think

Use office dots as the basis for this response tool as well.

Have kids brainstorm some thoughts they might have as they read a passage of Scripture. Their thoughts might include, "That's hard," "I'm surprised!" "That makes me feel peaceful," or "I'm confused." As kids brainstorm, encourage them to make a face that would indicate that thought, and let them look around at one another's expressions. Then give each child a sheet of office dots and a fine-line black marker or pen. Have them draw a face that shows each thought, encouraging them to cartoon creatively so they will have several stickers for each category of thought.

Encourage kids to use these dots as they read their Bibles on their own. Sometimes their responses to the Scripture may change over time, such as when they are initially confused but then ask some questions to help them understand better. They can then add another sticker to show how they are growing, or cover up the first sticker to show their confusion has been answered.

School Year Theme Verse

This is a great activity to do just after kids get their school pictures.

Have each child bring in a school picture. Encourage students to choose verses they believe offer special messages to them for this school year. For example, if a student is struggling with self-control at school, he or she might choose the encouragement of Romans 8:9a. If school seems especially hard, a child might choose 2 Corinthians 4:1. Help kids to use a concordance or topical index for ideas. (For younger children, you may wish to select several verses that seem appropriate for school, such as Luke 2:52 or Daniel 1:17a, so they are not overwhelmed by having the whole Bible to choose from.)

When kids decide on special verses to guide them through the year, have them each note the verse and place his or her school picture between the pages as a reminder of the chosen theme, and an easy way to locate it for reading again and again. (You can use the same procedure for holding the picture in the Bible as described in "Picture Perfect Verses" on p. 81.) If kids do this several years in a row, it will become a remarkable record of God's work in their lives.

Accordion to the Word...

To emphasize a list such as the Ten Commandments, the Beatitudes, or the fruit of the Spirit, or a sequence of events from a story, give kids a 2x11-inch strip of drawing paper. Have them accordion fold the paper so they have the same number of folds as items they want to remember.

Have them write or draw the items in sequence, one in each space between folds, leaving the first space blank. Show them how to apply glue on both sides of the edge of the paper and push the blank space down in between the pages where the original reference is so that the accordion book will be held in their Bibles.

Magnifying the Scripture

You'll need several Bible translations, one or more magnifying glasses, and a dictionary for this activity. Write Psalm 34:3 (NASB, below) on the chalkboard or on a large sheet of paper.

"O magnify the Lord with me, and let us exalt his name together."

Say: **Sometimes we can get a lot of understanding through doing a study of a particular word within a verse. We're going to look at the word "magnify" as an example.** Have kids use the magnifying glass to look up the word "magnify" in the dictionary and then explain what the magnifying glass does. Together read the verse from several different translations, noting other words that take the place of "magnify." Ask:

● **Why do people need things magnified?**

● **Based on what you know about magnification, what would be the results of the Lord being magnified?**

● **How would people joining together to magnify the Lord look?**

Have them strike a pose; then let them substitute the action they made up as they reread the verse. Ask:

● How does thinking about that one word help you to better understand and apply the verse?

● When might a word study be especially helpful as you read the Bible?

Encourage kids to use these steps of word study:

See (look for a keyword in the verse).

Search (find translations and definitions of the word, and ask yourself questions).

Substitute (read the definition or a statement of your understanding in place of the word in the verse).

Bible Vision

You'll need a video camera for these activities.

Challenge your kids to develop one or more sixty-second commercials for the Bible. Encourage them to develop their scripts based on research of significant passages that describe the Scripture. They might want to use testimonials from other kids or adults. By going through the research process and presenting the concepts in a limited time frame, your kids will do lots of evaluative thinking and analysis of exactly what about the Bible is most significant to their lives. If they do several commercials, they can organize their own Academy Awards, choosing the "best" commercial and gaining additional opportunity for analytical thinking. (Note: You'll want the whole group to develop the commercials so that it is an analysis of the idea rather than a competition between groups.)

If you don't have a video camera, you may have kids develop radio spots and record them on tape.

Current Events

Try this activity to help kids connect Bible principles to current events.

Have kids discuss a current news theme or story, recording facts and opinions about the story. Then have them think of a similar Bible story incident. Let them create a newscast about the current event, then create a follow-up report connected to a previous news story (the Bible story), similar to the format used by many television news magazine programs. A third element could be factual information about the topic. For example, the current story might be about a nation experiencing famine, the Bible story might be Joseph's reunion with his brothers, and the factual information component might be a report on world hunger statistics.

Videotape the presentations, and have kids take turns taking the program home to share with their families.

Bible Press Releases

Introduce kids to the concept of a press release. Say: **A press release is written information a company or organization gives to the media to announce an event or new product. It's short, factual information the media can use to develop a whole story if they choose to.**

Have kids write press releases about biblical events or stories as a way to sort out important facts. They could also write press releases about how a passage of Scripture is affecting their own lives, for example, one entitled *Romans 12 Hits the Sixth Grade Class.*

Want Ads

Have students find verses that tell how God wants us to live. There are many verses, so students will be able to choose different ones. Have students create want ads like they might find in the newspaper.

Say: **We are going to create a want ad page for a newspaper called "Heaven-Bound"** (or let students choose the name of a paper). **Here are some examples:**

Wanted: Thank offerings of all kinds. May be trouble-based; deliverance promised. "Sacrifice thank offerings to God, fulfill your vows to the Most High, and call upon me in the day of trouble; I will deliver you, and you will honor me" Psalm 50:14, 15 (NIV).

Wanted: Disciple makers, experience required. Own water tools not necessary. "Therefore go and make disciples of all nations, baptizing them in the name of the Father and of the Son and of the Holy Spirit" Matthew 28:19 (NIV).

Display the ads on a bulletin board, or have students take them home to hang in their rooms.

Signal Ahead

Help kids evaluate their life response to a lesson through this activity.

Say: **I'm giving each of you a postcard to address to yourself. On the back of the card, draw three circles in a line, like a traffic light. Color the top one red, the center one yellow, and the bottom one green. Under your traffic light, write something you think this week's Bible lesson teaches you to do. Make that your goal for this week. I will mail the postcard to you. When you receive it, decide whether your life has been a "Go" because you have really tried to do it, a "Caution" because you've struggled with your goal, or a "Stop" because you haven't remembered to try at all. No one will ask you what report you've given yourself; it's just a reminder to think about living the way you believe God wants you to.**

Standing Promises

You'll need multicolored, restickable notes.

Remind kids that a rainbow is a sign of God's covenant or promise and that the Bible is full of God's promises.

Give each student one restickable note of each color. Have each student put one of the notes on the inside cover of his or her Bible, then lay the second note one-half inch from the top of the first, and so on, until the student has a rainbow "minibook" to use as a promise book.

Say: **We're going to go on a promise hunt through God's Word. Whenever you find a promise, write it on one of the pages of your promise book. Keep your promise book with your Bible, and add to it whenever you read your Bible.**

Word Pictures

Choose a Bible concept word such as "love" or "joy," and have children develop a stylistic alphabet to write the word. What does "love" look like? What does "suffering" or "sorrow" look like? Encourage them to consider color as well as the form of the letters. Have them write the word, then surround it with Scripture references that relate to the concept they illustrated with word art.

Bible Boxes

Re-create a three-dimensional biblical scene on a small scale. For example, read about the tabernacle in the Old Testament, and then have students create a replica using different-sized grocery boxes. Also provide paper and tape for paper sculpting. Paint the scenes according to the scriptural details. This can be done with numerous scenes such as Noah's ark, the stable, the Crucifixion, or the empty tomb.

Natural Wonders

Use reference tools to study the wild flowers mentioned in the Bible. Some Bibles contain a listing of these. Gather local wild flowers, and dry them between two sheets of tissue paper.

Cut 8¹/₂x11-inch paper into half sheets. Fold these half sheets in half again, to look like greeting cards. Glue the dried flowers to the front to create decorative note paper. Choose a verse that you discovered during your search, write it on the inside, and send the cards to a person who is shut-in.

Spiritual Vitamins

You'll need an empty pill bottle for each child, paper, pens, and a topical Bible.

Say: **We need spiritual vitamins as well as vitamins for our physical needs. We can get them by reading God's Word daily and spending time in prayer. Use the topical Bible to find verses that encourage you. Write the references on slips of paper, and place them in your empty vitamin bottle. We will start our vitamin hunt in class, but continue adding to your list of spiritual vitamins when you do your study at home. Whenever you are feeling a little discouraged, open the bottle and take out a spiritual vitamin. Read the verse, and let it give you spiritual energy.**

Bible Journals

Reproduce the Bible-size page inserts (pp. 90–91) to encourage your kids to record their journey through God's Word.

Write down the verses you read, and choose a face that tells how it made you feel
(or draw one of your own on the blank face!).

DATE:	TODAY I READ:	IT MADE ME FEEL:					
		Happy	Mad	Sad	Excited	Confused	
		☺	😠	☹	😃	😕	◯
		☺	😠	☹	😃	😕	◯
		☺	😠	☹	😃	😕	◯
		☺	😠	☹	😃	😕	◯
		☺	😠	☹	😃	😕	◯
		☺	😠	☹	😃	😕	◯
		☺	😠	☹	😃	😕	◯

JOURNEY JOURNAL

Here's what I read:

Here's how it made me feel:

Here's what I'd like to say to God about this passage:

Here's how I can see this passage connected to my life:

Appendix

MULTIPLE INTELLIGENCES

LINGUISTIC INTELLIGENCE

Linguistic intelligence is the ability to understand and use language as a learning tool. Children who have this intelligence may like to read or write, but they may also like to give debate or speeches. They enjoy the meanings of words and they find satisfaction in expressing themselves through language.

LOGICAL-MATHEMATICAL INTELLIGENCE

People with a strong sense of logical-mathematical intelligence understand cause-and-effect relationships. They want to know how things work, and they ask a lot of questions. They enjoy logical outcomes and derive satisfaction from numbers and equations.

MUSICAL INTELLIGENCE

Musical people find meaning and will seek to express themselves in the patterns, tones, and rhythms of music. Some people with a strong musical intelligence are performers of music. Some are composers of music. And some find great meaning in simply listening to music.

INTERPERSONAL INTELLIGENCE

Interpersonal people are social people. They understand and empathize with people. They're comfortable in both large and small social settings. They're great discussers, and they find great significance in activities that allow them to interact with others.

REFLECTIVE INTELLIGENCE

People with a strong sense of reflective (or intrapersonal) intelligence are grounded in a profound sense of self-understanding. These people are independent and like to work alone. They're introspective and enjoy getting in touch with themselves and understanding their own motives.

BODILY-KINESTHETIC INTELLIGENCE

Bodily-kinesthetic intelligence refers to the ability to use body skills to solve problems or as a means of self-expression. People who are strong in this intelligence enjoy pursuits such as sports, dancing, crafts, and acting. They like to touch things and gain meaning from various textures. You may find that children with this intelligence fidget or move around a lot in class.

VISUAL-SPATIAL INTELLIGENCE

This is the ability to understand space relationships. They're good at manipulating space the way an architect does. People with strong visual-spatial intelligence have a good sense of direction-they're natural navigators. And they express themselves well in visual arts such as painting or film. These people need to see things to understand them.

NATURALISTIC INTELLIGENCE

People with this intelligence have the ability to recognize patterns in nature. They easily understand the differences between various plants or animals. These people may collect rocks or plants or bugs and may organize them according to their similarities or differences. These people enjoy any activity that allows them to explore the natural world.

Group Publishing, Inc.
Attention: Product Development
P.O. Box 481
Loveland, CO 80539
Fax: (970) 679-4370

Evaluation for
The Ultimate Bible Guide for Children's Ministry

Please help Group Publishing, Inc., continue to provide innovative and useful resources for ministry. Please take a moment to fill out this evaluation and mail or fax it to us. Thanks!

● ● ●

1. As a whole, this book has been (circle one)

not very helpful   very helpful

1   2   3   4   5   6   7   8   9   10

2. The best things about this book:

3. Ways this book could be improved:

4. Things I will change because of this book:

5. Other books I'd like to see Group publish in the future:

6. Would you be interested in field-testing future Group products and giving us your feedback? If so, please fill in the information below:

Name _____

Street Address _____

City _____ State _____ Zip _____

Phone Number _____ Date _____

Group's
hands-On
BiBLE
curriculum™

BRING THE BIBLE TO LIFE FOR YOUR 1ST- THROUGH 6TH-GRADERS...
WITH GROUP'S HANDS-ON BIBLE CURRICULUM™
Energize your kids with Active Learning!

Group's **Hands-On Bible Curriculum**™ will help you teach the Bible in a radical new way. It's based on Active Learning—the same teaching method Jesus used.

In each lesson, students will participate in exciting and memorable learning experiences using fascinating gadgets and gizmos you've not seen with any other curriculum. Your elementary students will discover biblical truths and <u>remember</u> what they learn because they're <u>doing</u> instead of just listening.

You'll save time and money, too!

While students are learning more, you'll be working less—simply follow the quick and easy instructions in the **Teacher Guide**. You'll get tons of material for an energy-packed 35- to 60-minute lesson. And, if you have extra time, there's an arsenal of Bonus Ideas and Time Stuffers to keep kids occupied—and learning! Plus, you'll SAVE BIG over other curriculum programs that require you to buy expensive separate student books—all student handouts in Group's **Hands-On Bible Curriculum** are photocopiable!

In addition to the easy-to-use **Teacher Guide**, you'll get all the essential teaching materials you need in a ready-to-use **Learning Lab**®. No more running from store to store hunting for lesson materials—all the active-learning tools you need to teach 13 exciting Bible lessons to any size class are provided for you in the **Learning Lab**.

Challenging topics each quarter keep your kids coming back!

Group's **Hands-On Bible Curriculum** covers topics that matter to your kids and teaches them the Bible with integrity. Switching topics every month keeps your 1st- through 6th-graders enthused and coming back for more. The full two-year program will help your kids...

•make God-pleasing decisions,
•recognize their God-given potential, and
•seek to grow as Christians.

Take the boredom out of Sunday school, children's church, and midweek meetings for your elementary students. Make your job easier and more rewarding with no-fail lessons that are ready in a flash. Order Group's **Hands-On Bible Curriculum** for your 1st- through 6th-graders today.

Hands-On Bible Curriculum is also available for
Toddlers & 2s, Preschool, and Pre-K and K!

Order today from your local Christian bookstore, or write: Group Publishing, P.O. Box 485, Loveland, CO 80539.

Exciting Resources for Your Children's Ministry

No-Miss Lessons for Preteen Kids

Getting the attention of 5th- and 6th-graders can be tough. Meet the challenge with these 22 faith-building, active-learning lessons that deal with self-esteem...relationships...making choices...and other topics. Perfect for Sunday school, meeting groups, lock-ins, and retreats!

ISBN 0-7644-2015-1

The Children's Worker's Encyclopedia of Bible-Teaching Ideas

New ideas—and lots of them!—for captivating children with stories from the Bible. You get over 340 attention-grabbing, active-learning devotions...art and craft projects...creative prayers...service projects... field trips...music suggestions...quiet reflection activities...skits...and more—winning ideas from each and every book of the Bible! Simple, step-by-step directions and handy indexes make it easy to slide an idea into any meeting—on short notice—with little or no preparation!

Old Testament   ISBN 1-55945-622-1
New Testament   ISBN 1-55945-625-6

"Show Me!" Devotions for Leaders to Teach Kids

Susan L. Lingo

Here are all the eye-catching science tricks, stunts, and illusions that kids love learning so they can flabbergast adults...but now there's an even *better* reason to know them! Each amazing trick is an illustration for an "Oh, Wow!" devotion that drives home a memorable Bible truth. Your children will learn how to share these devotions with others, too!

ISBN 0-7644-2022-4

Fun & Easy Games

With these 89 games, your children will *cooperate* instead of compete—so everyone finishes a winner! That means no more hurt feelings...no more children feeling like losers...no more hovering over the finish line to be sure there's no cheating. You get new games to play in gyms...classrooms...outside on the lawn...and as you travel!

ISBN 0-7644-2042-9

Order today from your local Christian bookstore, or write:
Group Publishing, P.O. Box 485, Loveland, CO 80539.